Culture and Society at Lullingstone Roman Villa

Caroline K. Mackenzie

Archaeopress Publishing Ltd
Summertown Pavilion
18-24 Middle Way
Summertown
Oxford OX2 7LG

www.archaeopress.com

ISBN 978-1-78969-290-7
ISBN 978-1-78969-291-4 (e-Pdf)

© C K Mackenzie and Archaeopress 2019

Cover: Lullingstone Villa in its landscape in the later fourth century AD (illustration by Peter Urmston). © Historic England Archive.

All rights reserved. No part of this book may be reproduced, or transmitted, in any form or by any means, electronic, mechanical, photocopying or otherwise, without the prior written permission of the copyright owners.

This book is available direct from Archaeopress or from our website www.archaeopress.com

For my parents and Jock

and in loving memory of Mrs Margaret Barrowcliff MBE

Contents

List of Figures ii

Preface and Acknowledgements v

Chapter One: Introduction 1

Chapter Two: The villa within its landscape setting and the role of topography in the owner's self-representation 5
    Landscape setting.. 5
    Ancillary buildings 14
        Circular shrine and temple-mausoleum 14
        Granary 16
    Comparable villas 20
    A further case study: Chedworth 22

Chapter Three: The choice and use of mosaics in the fourth century villa: how the patron presented his cultural identity and status through pavements 24
    Grand designs... 24
    The central room 25
        The seasons 26
        Bellerophon 29
    The apse 31
        Europa and the bull 35
        The inscription 37
        An incongruous combination? 40
    Classical literature in other Romano-British villas............................ 41

Chapter Four: Additional reconstructions of the villa 44
    The villa within its landscape setting 44
    The villa's interior space and decoration 46
    Summary of reconstructions 52

Chapter Five: Conclusion 53

Bibliography.. 55
    Online sources 57

List of Figures

Villa plan showing all the construction phases. © Historic England Archive vi

Figure 1.1. Chi Rho wall-painting, Lullingstone. c. AD 380. © 2019 The Trustees of the British Museum.. 2

Figure 1.2. 'Orantes' wall-painting, Lullingstone. c. AD 380. © 2019 The Trustees of the British Museum.. 3

Figure 2.1. North Kent in the Roman period. From Wilson 2009: 26. © Historic England Archive. 6

Figure 2.2. Lullingstone Villa in its landscape in the later fourth century AD (illustration by Peter Urmston). © Historic England Archive................................ 7

Figure 2.3. Dig at Otford, Church Field. 30.7.18. Photograph: by author. 8

Figure 2.4. Illustration of Villa c. AD 90-100 (illustration by Peter Urmston). © Historic England Archive. 9

Figure 2.5. Baths: view looking north-west, steps in background. Meates 1979: 203, Plate XIXa. © Kent Archaeological Society. 10

Figure 2.6. Baths: close-up view of steps looking west. Meates 1979: 203, Plate XIXb. © Kent Archaeological Society. 10

Figure 2.7. The baths as they may have appeared in the late third century AD (illustration by Peter Dunn/Richard Lea). © Historic England Archive................... 11

Figure 2.8. Deep Room: niche in south wall showing painting of water-nymphs. Meates 1979: 186, plate Vd. © Kent Archaeological Society.................................. 11

Figure 2.9. Reconstruction of 'Deep Room' shown at underground level, c. AD 380 (illustration by Peter Dunn/Richard Lea). © Historic England Archive................ 12

Figure 2.10. Modern view of Darent Valley, taken in field behind Lullingstone Villa. Photograph: by author. 13

Figure 2.11. Modern view of Darent Valley, taken from modern road approaching the Villa. Photograph: by author. 13

Figure 2.12. Reconstruction drawing of Lullingstone Villa in the fourth century AD (illustration by Alan Sorrell). © Historic England Archive...................................... 14

Figure 2.13. Lullingstone Villa with temple-mausoleum behind, in the late third century AD (illustration by Peter Urmston). © Historic England Archive. 15

Figure 2.14. Granary: view looking north-east. Meates 1979: 207, Plate XXIIIa. © Kent Archaeological Society.. 17

Figure 2.15. Granary: central boxes. Meates 1979: 208, Plate XXIVa. © Kent Archaeological Society. 18

Figure 2.16. Middle Littleton Tithe Barn, a thirteenth century barn in Evesham, Worcestershire. © National Trust Images/Robert Morris.. 19

Figure 2.17. Remains of Great Witcombe Roman Villa, Gloucestershire. © Historic England Archive. 21

Figure 2.18. Reconstruction drawing of Great Witcombe Roman Villa in the fourth century AD (illustration by Ivan Lapper). © Historic England Archive................... 21

Figure 2.19. An illustration showing an aerial view of Chedworth Roman Villa as it was in its peak. © National Trust Images. 23

Figure 3.1. Detail: Bellerophon on Pegasus, spearing the Chimaera. c. AD 330-60. © Historic England Archive. 26

Figure 3.2. Detail: Summer. c. AD 330-60. © Historic England Archive. 27

Figure 3.3. Brading Roman Villa mosaic: Spring. © Oglander Roman Trust. 28

Figure 3.4. Brading Roman Villa mosaic: Summer. © Oglander Roman Trust. 28

Figure 3.5. Brading Roman Villa mosaic: Winter. © Oglander Roman Trust................ 28

Figure 3.6. Detail of Pegasus and the Chimaera, Hinton St Mary. Early fourth century AD. © 2019 The Trustees of the British Museum... 30

Figure 3.7. Tombstone of Julia Velva depicting apsidal dining room, AD 200-300. (YORYM: 1998.25). © York Museums Trust (Yorkshire Museum). 31

Figure 3.8. Reconstruction of Lullingstone's apsidal dining room with stibadium. c. AD 330-60 (illustration by Peter Dunn). © Historic England Archive...................... 32

Figure 3.9. View across central audience chamber to apse with step (looking south). Meates 1979: 201, Plate XVIIb. © Kent Archaeological Society............................... 33

Figure 3.10. View across central audience chamber to apse with step (looking north-west). Meates 1979: 201, Plate XVIIc. © Kent Archaeological Society. 33

Figure 3.11. Reconstruction of Lullingstone's audience chamber and apse. c. AD 330-60 (illustration by Peter Dunn). © Historic England Archive. 34

Figure 3.12. Europa mosaic. c. AD 330-60. © Historic England Archive. 36

Figure 3.13. Detail: Cupid. c. AD 330-60. © Historic England Archive............................ 36

Figure 3.14. Europa mosaic. Keynsham. Fourth century AD. © www.bathnewseum.com ... 37

Figure 3.15. Otford wall-painting and inscription. Early second century AD. © 2019 The Trustees of the British Museum. 41

Figure 3.16. Scenes from Virgil's Aeneid. Low Ham mosaic, fourth century AD. © Somerset Archaeological and Natural History Society and South West Heritage Trust, 2019... 43

Figure 4.1. View of Lullingstone Roman Villa from south-east. (3D Reconstruction with Modo Software.) © Rob Sherratt 45

Figure 4.2. View of Lullingstone Roman Villa from north-east. (3D Reconstruction with Modo Software.) © Rob Sherratt 45

Figure 4.3. View of Lullingstone Roman Villa from south-west. (3D Reconstruction with Modo Software.) © Rob Sherratt 46

Figure 4.4. The floorplan of the whole villa. © Rod Shelton. 47
Figure 4.5. The front of the villa including the veranda (from the east). © Rod Shelton. 47
Figure 4.6. The audience chamber. © Rod Shelton. 48
Figure 4.7. The audience chamber, with the apsidal dining room beyond. © Rod Shelton 49
Figure 4.8. The bath complex at the south of the villa, including the well. © Rod Shelton 50
Figure 4.9. The house-church at the north of the villa. © Rod Shelton 50
Figure 4.10. The Deep Room seen beneath the floorboards of the room above it. © Rod Shelton 51

Preface and Acknowledgements

Dr David Davison at Archaeopress was instrumental in evolving my work into this final publication. I am very grateful to him for all his enthusiasm and advice and for committing to the project. Thank you also to Patrick Harris, Dan Stott, Ben Heaney and everyone at Archaeopress for all their hard work. We are delighted that we are able to publish this book in 2019 to coincide with the celebrations marking the 70-year anniversary of the commencement of excavations at the site. These celebratory events include a reunion of many of the volunteers who helped in the original excavations of this extraordinary Villa.

The origin of this publication lies in a dissertation which I completed in 2018 for a Master of Arts in Classical Art and Archaeology at King's College London. I should like to thank Dr John Pearce for all his help and guidance at that time. He introduced me to a vast and varied corpus of work on Roman Britain and patiently steered me through my research, kindly reading drafts of my dissertation and providing valuable comments. Thank you also to Dr Will Wootton for all that he taught me about mosaics, which enabled me to consider Lullingstone from a wider perspective. Dr Zena Kamash offered much encouragement and support both in relation to my dissertation and also this book.

I should like to thank Professor David Breeze for reading and commenting on an early draft of the book. Thank you to Kevin Fromings, Project Leader of Discover Roman Otford Project (DROP) for welcoming me to the dig in Church Field, just a few miles from Lullingstone, and for all his support. Thank you also to Dr Gerald Cramp, President of Kent Archaeological Society (KAS) for all his encouragement and for sharing his account of the excavations at Lullingstone (at which he volunteered while still a young schoolboy). On a specific note, I am grateful to him for clarifying that the flood to which I refer on page 10 was caused by a cloudburst.

I should also like to thank the team at Lullingstone Roman Villa, Emma Freeman (Site Manager), Alison Lowe (Historic Property Steward) and Simon Price-Johnson (Historic Property Steward) who always gave me a warm welcome at the villa and willingly shared their knowledge, resources and time.

I am grateful to the individuals, museums and societies who have kindly given permission for their images to be included. Formal credits appear with the respective images. A special thank you to Rod Shelton and Rob Sherratt for the images of their respective reconstructions of the villa. Thank you also for all the support I have received from The Friends of Brading Roman Villa, in particular David Reeves and Robert Pitts.

Most important of all, thank you to my family and especially to Grannie, my sister, Liz, my nephew, Tom, my parents, and my husband, Jock. Thank you, all, for everything.

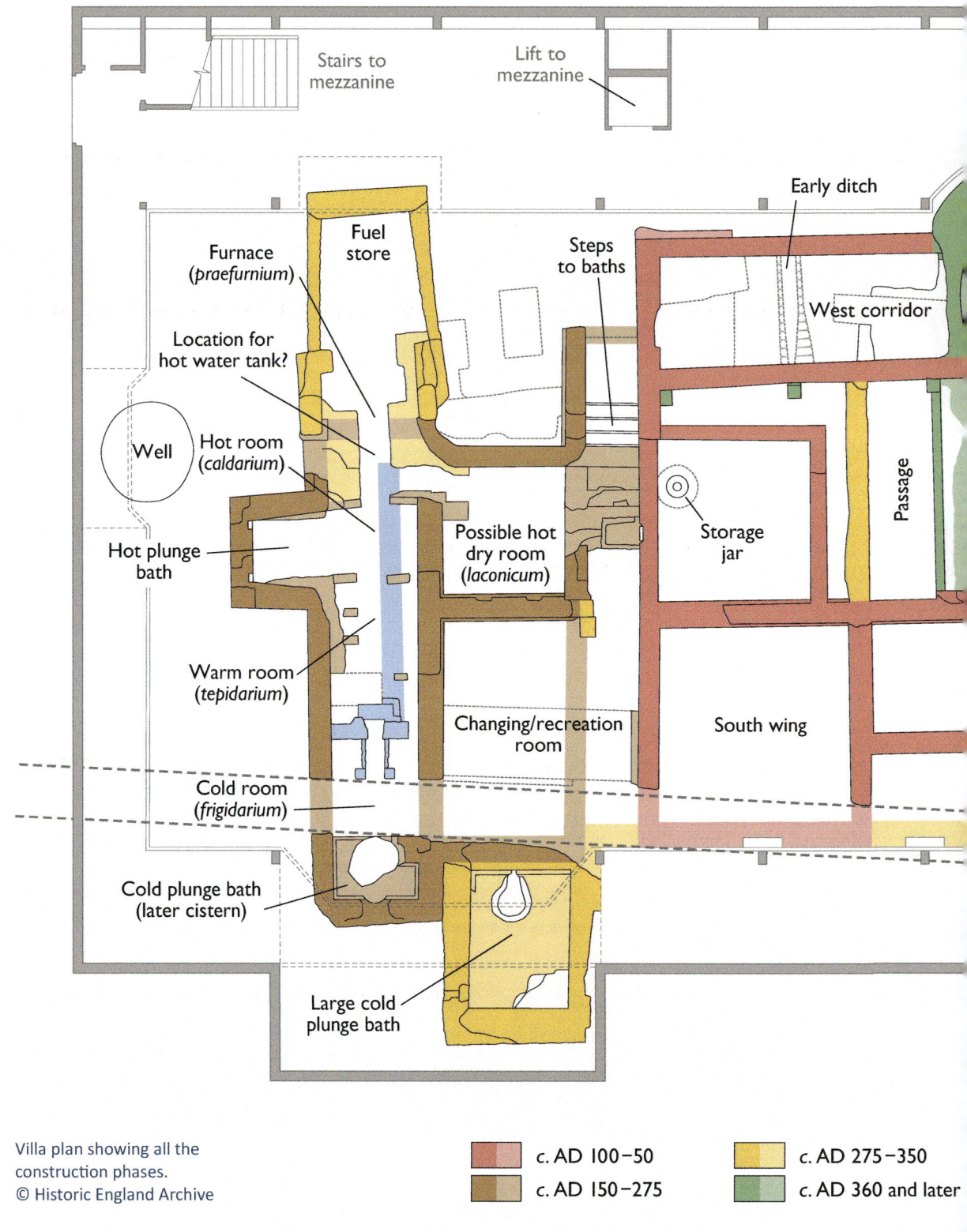

Villa plan showing all the construction phases.
© Historic England Archive

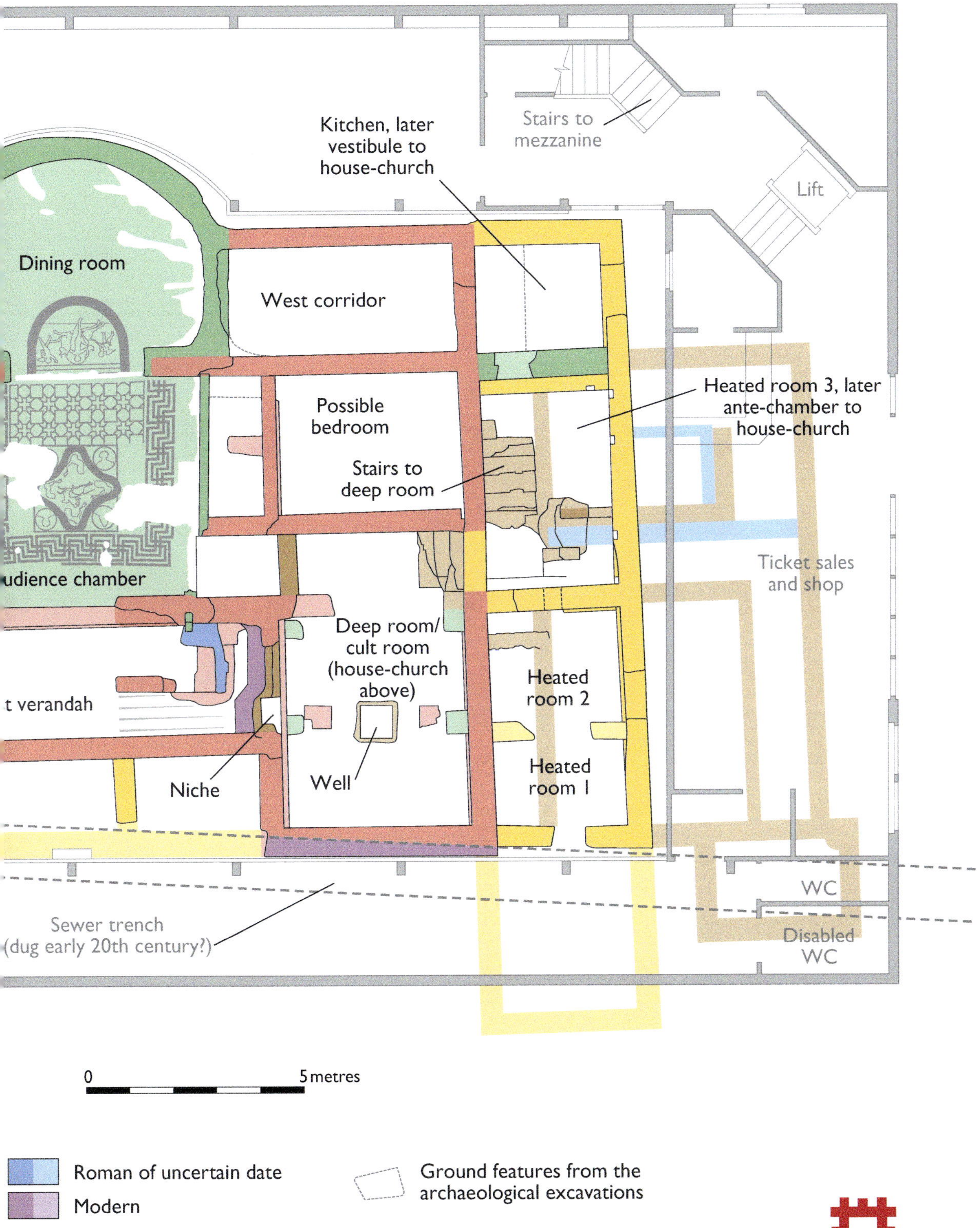

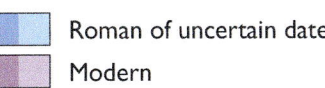
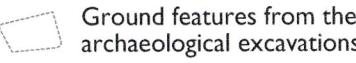

Chapter One

Introduction

In 1788 the first clues as to the existence of a Roman site in the vicinity of Lullingstone in the Darent Valley, Kent were recorded by John Thorpe in his work *Custumale Roffense*. He reported various discoveries of Roman coins and that in about 1750 when the fence around Lullingstone deer park was being renewed, diggers of the post holes had struck a mosaic. While all this had suggested Roman occupation, Thorpe's main interest lay instead in the dilapidated church of Lullingstane, believed by Thorpe to have been built in Saxon times. It was not until 1939 that an archaeological survey undertaken by Ernest Greenfield and Edwyn Birchenough of the Darent Valley Archaeological Research Group concentrated on the Roman finds and that the remarkable story of the discovery of Lullingstone Roman Villa properly began.[1]

The Second World War halted the 1939 survey which had to be put on hold until 1947 when the archaeological team was joined by Lieutenant-Colonel Geoffrey Meates, recently retired from the Royal Artillery and now resident in the gatehouse at Lullingstone Castle.[2] Meates reports of the initial investigations: 'Among the tangle of undergrowth with which the area was covered lay one or two fallen trees. Among the roots of one of these trees was found Roman pottery and fragments of tile, and this endorsed the opinion of the investigators that here might lie hidden the remains of a Roman building.'

Excavations formally commenced in 1949 and these revealed the remains of a Roman villa which boasted much evidence of a luxurious lifestyle: mosaics, sculpture, wall-painting, a hypocaust and baths. By 1955, Meates had become leader of the excavations and he oversaw them until their completion in 1961, documenting the finds in a series of publications.[3] The team was meticulous in its recovery of the fragmented painted wall plaster which, when assembled, produced what are now some of the best-known wall-paintings from Roman Britain. An image of the Chi Rho [fig. 1.1] and a portrayal of figures in the 'orantes' pose [fig. 1.2] indicated that Christian worship had taken place here. Lullingstone is widely cited as a very rare example of a plausible house-church used for liturgical purposes. Further, the Christian house-church was believed to have been built above, and used simultaneously as, a pagan cult room. So far, this is a unique discovery in Roman Britain, if not the empire, and is one of the most widely discussed aspects of Lullingstone.

Such is the deemed importance of the painted plaster fragments that they are displayed at the British Museum. The evidence of religion at Lullingstone has been exploited and applied to the mosaics in the adjacent rooms. While the religious interpretation is of undeniable importance to any study of the villa, there are other factors relevant to its history. This book interprets the evidence in other ways and asks questions

---

[1] Meates 1979: 15.
[2] Wilson 2009: 3 and 36.
[3] Meates: 1951, 1952, 1953, 1955, 1963, 1979 and 1987.

Figure 1.1. Chi Rho wall-painting, Lullingstone. c. AD 380. © 2019 The Trustees of the British Museum.

based instead on the use of space, landscape setting and architectural context of the mosaics. Wallace-Hadrill's work in Pompeii and Herculaneum focused on the use of domestic space and the public and private spheres of a home.[4] He suggested we might learn about the social standing of the inhabitants not only by examining the way they adorned their homes and making inferences from that, but also by considering how they were using their houses to create and assert their cultural and socio-economic identity. Wallace-Hadrill also examined the depth of a house with multiple reception rooms enabling the owner to discriminate between visitors, with limited access only to the innermost areas.[5] Such 'access analysis' can also be used when examining the spatial syntax of Lullingstone's reception rooms. Scott subsequently applied a similar concept to the interior space of Romano-British villas and extended it by placing more emphasis on the landscape setting.[6]

This book explores and examines how Lullingstone's inhabitants used domestic space to assert their status and cultural identity. There are good examples of how, by alluding to knowledge of Graeco-Roman culture, villa-owners expressed their *paideia*: their appreciation of literature, philosophy and mythology enjoyed by the Roman élite.[7] In what follows, 'domestic space' encompasses the architectural layout

---

[4] Wallace-Hadrill 1988.
[5] Wallace-Hadrill 1988: 52-55.
[6] Scott 2000.
[7] Scott 2000: 126-8.

Figure 1.2. 'Orantes' wall-painting, Lullingstone. c. AD 380. © 2019 The Trustees of the British Museum.

of the villa, including the positioning of the rooms used for receiving visitors and entertaining guests. Ellis' study of the use of Classical reception rooms in Romano-British houses provides a useful basis on which to examine how Lullingstone's inhabitants adopted Roman architecture and potentially the social customs which went with it.[8] He cautions that the educated Romano-British élite often re-interpreted Roman art to suit their own requirements.[9] Witts challenged some of Ellis' conclusions and demonstrated that we should look carefully at the precise layout of mosaics before jumping to conclusions about their function.[10] This book therefore considers the mosaics' orientation within rooms and the proportion of space occupied by the figurative parts, compared to walkways and spaces for furniture.

Given much material is still in situ, it is possible to explore the interior space and landscape in person and consider the evidence experientially, carrying out one's own viewshed survey on foot. Tilley's innovative 1994 book was based on such an approach.[11] This experience enables us to examine the relative prominence of the villa and its ancillary buildings; for example, were they highly visible in the landscape? We can also consider how the architects combined the setting with the layout of the

---

[8] Ellis 1995.
[9] Ellis 1995: 165.
[10] Witts 2000.
[11] Tilley: 1994.

villa to create a conspicuous display of the owner's standing and worth. All this is considered in Chapter Two.

Chapter Three focuses on the mosaics, dated c. AD 330-360 at a time of the villa's improvement and expansion. It investigates the scenes commissioned by the patrons, and the impact of the images on various viewers. Scholars have emphasised the importance of considering individual responses to ancient art and the subjective nature of these reactions.[12] To do this more fully than previous interpretations of Lullingstone, we need to consider as wide as possible a range of visitors to a villa on a rural settlement, which might naturally have included tenant farmers and workers as well as those guests invited to the villa's more private spaces. This book also challenges one scholar's assertion that mosaics were commonly chosen in 'random and non-significant combinations'.[13] The latter hypothesis assumes patrons' over-reliance on pattern books and a standard mythological repertoire; but, by ignoring the architectural and archaeological context of such décor, this approach is too reductionist.[14] Chapter Three therefore solicits whether we have compelling evidence that the Lullingstone mosaics were the product of a deliberate and informed choice.[15]

This book examines the practices of the inhabitants primarily during the late third and fourth centuries AD and how they adopted Roman culture in their domestic space. By way of comparison, it briefly considers the interior and exterior spaces of some contemporary Romano-British villas to assess whether Lullingstone was typical, or exceptional.

---

[12] Elsner 2007.
[13] Ling 1991: 148.
[14] Scott 2000: 114-7.
[15] Perring 2003: 103.

Chapter Two

The villa within its landscape setting and the role of topography in the owner's self-representation

Landscape setting

While Chapter Three focuses on the mosaics, we should resist evaluating provincial art in isolation without considering its archaeological context.[1] Scholars have warned against a 'myopic' approach to excavation where the villa's wider spatial context receives little assessment.[2] This chapter, therefore, considers the villa in its landscape setting. Recent studies have focused on the role of topography in villa-owners' self-representation and as a means of displaying wealth and status.[3] So far, this has not been applied in any detail to Lullingstone. Using Tilley's approach (mentioned in Chapter One) we can explore the landscape on foot to experience the visual impact of monuments: 'As we move around in space, our perspective of the landscape alters... The monuments... are then about establishing *control* over topographic perspective'.[4] We can then ask what claims the Lullingstone owner was making as to his control of the landscape. In a recent case study on Roman barrows and their landscape context at Bartlow, Cambridgeshire,[5] GIS (a Geographic Information System) was used to test whether the burial mounds (barrows) were visible from nearby roads, barrows and villas. Bearing all this in mind, this chapter describes the setting of the villa today and considers how it might have appeared to a visitor to the Roman villa.

Lullingstone Roman Villa is in the Darent Valley in west Kent and is managed by English Heritage. The villa sits on a terrace cut into the hillside 55m west of the west bank of the River Darent, whose valley cuts through the North Downs, and was around 20 miles from *Londinium* (London). Richborough and Dover, both 70 miles away from Lullingstone on the coast, were major ports of entry. From here, the main route of Watling Street (our modern A2) crossed the Darent Valley 5 miles north of Lullingstone, leading north-west to London, and serving both the army and the administration [fig. 2.1].[6] A valley road (not yet found)[7] probably passed through neighbouring estates - Otford, Shoreham, Lullingstone, Farningham and Darent - before joining Watling Street.

Lullingstone was a favourable site because of its access to varied resources and agricultural riches. The river provided a constant source of water, which may have been used to power corn mills. Flat bottomed boats could have navigated the river

---

[1] Scott 2000: 14.
[2] Taylor 2011: 182.
[3] Scott 2000, 2004 and 2012; Taylor 2011.
[4] Tilley 1994: 204.
[5] Eckardt et al. 2009.
[6] Meates 1963: 4; Wilson 2009: 26.
[7] Meates 1955: 122-3 and 1987: 2.

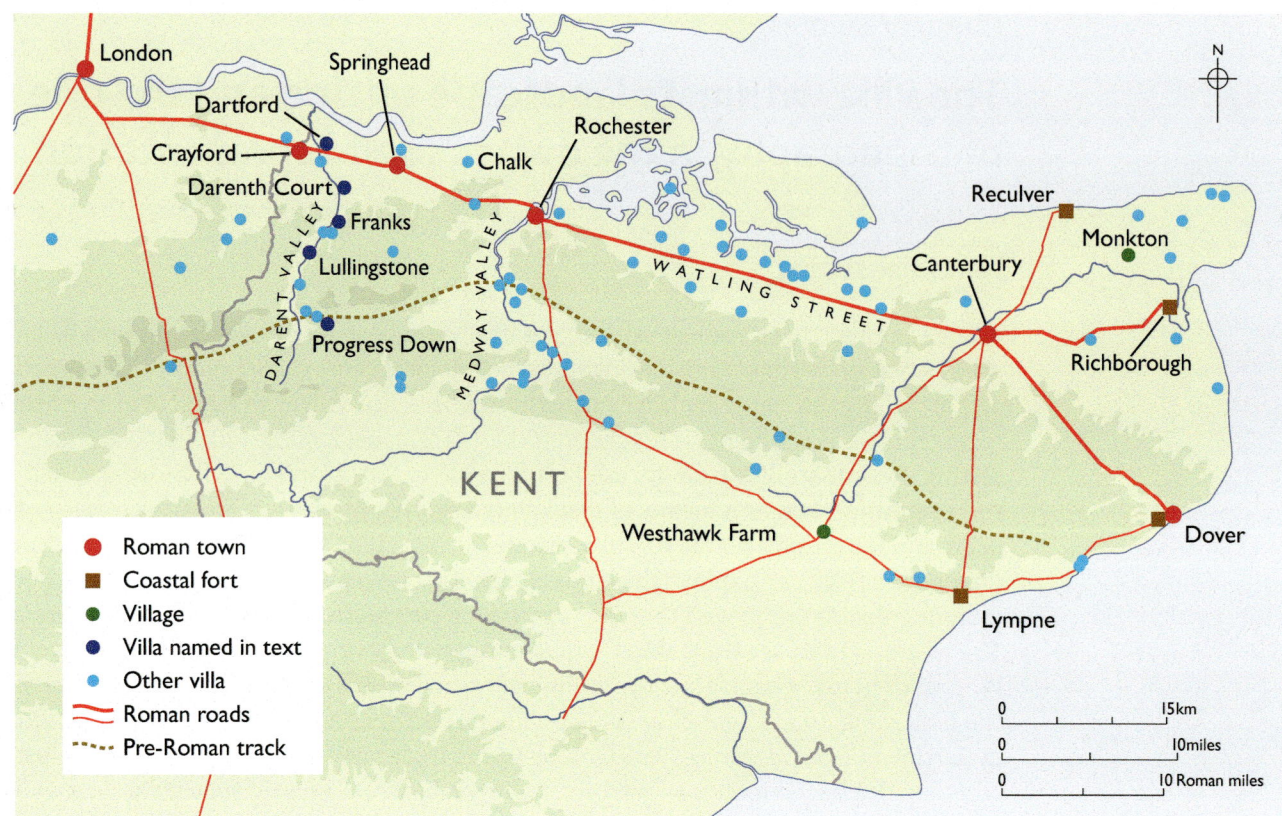

Figure 2.1. North Kent in the Roman period. From Wilson 2009: 26. © Historic England Archive.

down to the Thames Estuary (around 12.9 miles).[8] The river valley provided fertile soil for growing crops. Extensive woodland provided building timber and fuel. The hills behind the villa would have been ideal for grazing cattle and sheep. Thus, the villa was probably at a junction of different landscape zones enabling both arable and pastoral farming. An illustration communicates this aspect of the site well [fig. 2.2].

As in other areas of Kent and South-East England, intensive landscape exploitation, structured seemingly around villa estates, developed in the Darent Valley possibly related to changes in landholding. A London writing tablet shows use of Roman law to reinforce ownership rights on a Kent property, probably expropriated after conquest.[9] This could explain the evidence which has been found for buildings of significant size every two/three miles along the Darent Valley from Otford to Dartford.[10] These may have formed self-contained farms of similar size with around ten villas in total.[11] Their relationship to the local farming population can be partially reconstructed by a map showing the Historic Environment Record (HER) information (see: http://webapps.kent.gov.uk/KCC.HeritageMaps.Web.Sites.Public/Default.aspx). This reveals Roman pits, implements, ditches, pottery and other monuments immediately surrounding the Darent villas. This suggests the landscape was populated by modest farming sites,

---

[8] Wilson 2009: 23.
[9] Tomlin 1996.
[10] Meates 1955: 2 and 1979: 15.
[11] Wilson 2009: 3.

Figure 2.2. Lullingstone Villa in its landscape in the later fourth century AD (illustration by Peter Urmston). © Historic England Archive.

exploited by the large villa estates which were channelling agricultural riches into villa display. However, Millett cautions against assuming conspicuous display was always funded from local sources.[12]

In total there are around sixty known/suspected villas in Kent, most of which are in north Kent. They fall into three main groups: along the line of Watling Street between Canterbury and Rochester; in the Medway Valley; and in the Darent Valley.[13] Darenth Court, 4 miles from Lullingstone, is one of largest villa complexes in the country, covering an area of around 2.6 hectares[14] with a large courtyard, baths, guest house and ornamental canal. It also included an aisled building possibly for the bailiff and workers with a separate bath house for them, and agricultural buildings.[15] Franks villa at Farningham was, like Lullingstone, occupied from the first to fifth centuries. There are three possible villas in Otford including Progress Down (see Chapter Three 'Classical literature in other Romano-British villas') and Church Field which is currently under excavation [fig. 2.3].

Lullingstone was therefore part of an intensively exploited and agriculturally rich landscape. The Darent Valley villas probably supplied food and other agricultural produce to London and provided residences for the London élites. The supply of the

[12] c.f. Hadrian's villa, Tivoli. Millett 1990: 97.
[13] Wilson 2009: 26.
[14] https://historicengland.org.uk/listing/the-list/list-entry/1012965 (27/8/18).
[15] Neal 1991: 21.

Figure 2.3. Dig at Otford, Church Field. 30.7.18. Photograph: by author.

food grown on their estates was facilitated by the near transport links (Watling Street and the River Darent)[16] providing connections to London and further afield. Pottery types made in North Kent in the second/third centuries AD have been discovered in settlements on the east coast of England as far north as Hadrian's Wall. Food produce from the Darent Valley villas might therefore also have been sent this far north.[17] In the fourth century, there is evidence of corn being exported to the continent.[18] A wealthy owner of Lullingstone was likely to have exploited all the above.

The site presented limitations and challenges for the builders. The land west of the west riverbank gently sloped upwards for about 55m before reaching a steep hillside. A terrace approximately 40m deep had to be created for the first phase of the villa, with the steep slope behind creating a protective backdrop. The villa itself stood between 0.915m and 1.22m above the gently sloping area to the east.[19] Before considering the later stages of the villa, and the changing landscape, let us briefly outline the various stages of construction. There is evidence for an early establishment at Lullingstone (c. AD 50-80) and in c. AD 90-100 a house was constructed in flint and mortar [fig. 2.4].[20] In c. AD 180 the house was expanded with baths added at the south, external kitchens at the west and cult rooms at the north. Meates suggested that the villa was then abandoned in c. AD 200 and not reoccupied until AD 280-290 when the baths were rebuilt but it is now believed that occupation was in fact continuous throughout the

---

[16] Fulford 2003: 1.
[17] Fulford 2003: 18.
[18] Casey 1994: 38.
[19] Meates 1979: 17.
[20] Meates 1955: xv.

Figure 2.4. Illustration of Villa c. AD 90-100 (illustration by Peter Urmston). © Historic England Archive.

third century.[21] In AD 330-360 an apsidal dining room with mosaics was added. In c. AD 380 the baths were dismantled and a Christian house-church was founded. A fire in the early fifth century led to the final abandonment of the villa.[22]

In the late second century expansion, some of the bank at the south of the villa was removed to construct the bath block whilst also taking advantage of the natural slope westward from the flood plain.[23] The baths were therefore a few feet lower than the rest of the villa, hence a staircase down into them [figs. 2.5-2.6]. To own private baths conferred status, as one could invite business contacts and friends to bathe whilst discussing politics, culture and work.[24] Following this remodelling, the house took on a new status and the river setting acquired even more significance, with water now a feature both inside and outside the villa. When the baths were constructed in c. AD 180, a well was dug to the south of the bath block, around 4.27 m from the exterior wall of the furnace.[25] This was used to supply water to the baths until the end of the second century, probably via a wooden aqueduct system. The existence of the latter was indicated by the discovery of a series of post-holes between the south walls of the villa and the well. The source of the water supply to the remodelled baths from the late third century onwards is unknown but the proximity of the river (around 61m to the east of the site of the well)[26] would have facilitated a similar aqueduct system [fig. 2.7].

---

[21] Wilson 2009: 40.
[22] Meates 1979: 18-9
[23] Meates 1979: 91.
[24] Esmonde Cleary 2013: 110-1.
[25] Meates 1979: 100.
[26] Meates 1979: 102.

Figure 2.5. Baths: view looking north-west, steps in background. Meates 1979: 203, Plate XIXa. © Kent Archaeological Society.

Figure 2.6. Baths: close-up view of steps looking west. Meates 1979: 203, Plate XIXb. © Kent Archaeological Society.

A symbolic dimension of the owner's appropriation of the landscape and its resources was the establishment of a cult room apparently relating to water deities complete with a niched wall-painting of three water-nymphs [fig. 2.8]. This was created c. AD 180, contemporaneous with the baths, and demonstrated the owner's reverence for water. It was located at the north-east of the villa, where the slope had been excavated to create what is known as the 'Deep Room' [fig. 2.9].[27] The niche was later blocked up and could have easily escaped the excavators' notice but, in a twist of fate, following a cloudburst the site flooded mid-excavations and dislodged the plaster concealing the

---

[27] Meates 1955: 59.

Figure 2.7. The baths as they may have appeared in the late third century AD (illustration by Peter Dunn/ Richard Lea). © Historic England Archive.

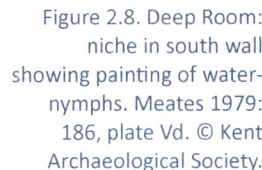

Figure 2.8. Deep Room: niche in south wall showing painting of water-nymphs. Meates 1979: 186, plate Vd. © Kent Archaeological Society.

Figure 2.9. Reconstruction of 'Deep Room' shown at underground level, c. AD 380 (illustration by Peter Dunn/Richard Lea). © Historic England Archive.

water-nymphs.[28] The villa-owner who created the water cult room might have seen this as a sign!

In c. AD 275, a wall was built across the east of the villa creating a veranda in which two east-west cross walls were discovered. These indicate the main entrance was via a central wooden staircase rising to the veranda but no other evidence of them has been found.[29] This position would also seem the most natural entrance in a previous period as it provided the grandest approach where the villa's symmetry and its framing by the hillside were clearly visible. Visitors would be invited to admire the villa's façade as they approached the entrance steps. The veranda's floor level was about 1.5m above ground level,[30] enhancing the grandeur.

Although there is no direct evidence for formal gardening at Lullingstone,[31] other sites, such as Chedworth and Fishbourne, have offered traces of formal gardens suggesting they were a desirable feature of affluent villas.[32] At Brading on the Isle of Wight, the remodelling of the villa complex in the fourth century AD included a courtyard landscaped as a formal garden, indicated by the discovery of a cultivation soil during the 2008 excavations.[33] Botanical evidence for cultivated fruit crop at Lullingstone was found in a kitchen pit containing numerous seeds, pips and stones, including sloe, bird-cherry and cherry-plum.[34]

[28] Meates 1979: 17 and 33.
[29] Wilson 2009: 13.
[30] Fulford 2003: 11.
[31] Wilson 2009: 23.
[32] https://www.english-heritage.org.uk/learn/story-of-england/romans/landscape/ (17/8/18). c.f. Frocester, Gloucestershire in Millett 2016: 706.
[33] Cunliffe 2013: 270.
[34] Meates 1979: 107.

The villa within its landscape setting 13

Figure 2.10. Modern view of Darent Valley, taken in field behind Lullingstone Villa. Photograph: by author.

Figure 2.11. Modern view of Darent Valley, taken from modern road approaching the Villa. Photograph: by author.

Visitors today may appreciate the tranquil setting and the view from the villa [figs. 2.10 and 2.11] but how far can we back-project this modern appreciation onto Roman visitors? Modern subjective assessments of 'a lovely setting' must be qualified - however, we know from Roman authors that observers then were sensitive to the aesthetics of views and this is not just a modern phenomenon (Ausonius: *Moselle*; Pliny the Younger: *Epistulae* 2.17). The Darent Valley landscape lends itself to display and visitors to Roman Lullingstone may have looked across the river to the east bank and extensive farmland beyond and been impressed by the scale of production and activity - a landscape of rural wealth with workers toiling in the fields. Most reconstructions of Lullingstone [figs. 2.2, 2.4, 2.7 and 2.9] convey subliminal messages of the golden age of Roman Britain. Bathed in sunlight, they evoke Italian landscapes; Sorrell's gloomy depiction [fig. 2.12] is exceptional.

Figure 2.12. Reconstruction drawing of Lullingstone Villa in the fourth century AD (illustration by Alan Sorrell). © Historic England Archive.

This illustration shows both the circular shrine and the temple-mausoleum's respective positions. However, the circular shrine is believed to have fallen into ruin following disuse in the third century.

Ancillary buildings

Whilst examining the landscape setting of the villa, it is essential to consider its ancillary buildings which, as we shall see, played an important role in the villa-owner's display of wealth and status.

Circular shrine and temple-mausoleum

In c. AD 100 a circular building was constructed on a prepared terrace 24.4.m northwest of the villa, with a doorway to the east and a wooden stairway from the lower level.[35] A flint and mortar construction with a thatched roof but no windows, it is thought to have been used for cult purposes until c. AD 180. This is the only ancillary building which retains any trace on the modern site. The slope is steep and the elevated shrine must have made an imposing statement: the terrace which was cut into the hill-slope was about 2.44m higher than the ground level at the north of the villa enabling the shrine to dominate the site.[36] It stood on a semi-circular area 6.4m from east to west at its widest and the shrine's most westerly curve was free-standing some 0.45m at its narrowest from the western slope. The proximity of the steeply

---

[35] Meates 1979: 119.
[36] Meates 1979: 119.

Figure 2.13. Lullingstone Villa with temple-mausoleum behind, in the late third century AD (illustration by Peter Urmston). © Historic England Archive.

rising slope immediately behind the shrine would have added to the drama. The interior diameter of the shrine was 4.72m and the walls rose to a height of around 2.44m.[37] The thatched roof was of conical construction, creating an impression of the shrine reaching even higher upwards. Standing to the north-west of the villa, it would have been clearly visible as visitors approached the entrance on the east wing of the villa, from where the shrine would have towered above the villa to its right [fig. 2.12].

It is believed to have fallen into ruin following disuse in the third century. However, the terrace on which it stood was extended to receive a temple-mausoleum in AD 300. This stood prominently around 6m above the ground to the west of the villa[38] and exemplifies skilful use of the hill-slope to create monumentality and visibility [fig. 2.13]. The building takes the form of a 12.2m square Romano-Celtic temple[39], comprising an external ambulatory and rectangular *cella* inside. Beneath this was a tomb chamber with two lead coffins and various grave goods. We do not know the identity of the couple buried but it may be the villa-owner and his wife, and the temple-mausoleum seems to have been created for this double burial. The excavators found evidence of the *cella* being constructed after the burials had been completed.[40] The *cella* walls rose to around 3.66 m high, on top of which a pentice roof covered the surrounding ambulatory. Further height was created by a dome, or quadripartite vault, ensuring maximum visibility on the landscape.

---

[37] Meates 1979: 120.
[38] Meates 1979: 17.
[39] Meates 1979: 122.
[40] Meates 1979: 125.

As the circular shrine had by this time fallen into disrepair, the temple-mausoleum would now preside over the villa site. It is another example of the landscape being exploited to assert the owner's status: 'an ostentatious, if pious, expression of wealth'.[41] The date of construction of the temple-mausoleum coincides with a major refurbishment to the villa and its surroundings, all of which demonstrated the wealth and aspirations of the owner. The bath complex had been rebuilt and extended in around AD 280 and, as discussed below, in AD 293-297 a large granary was constructed to the north-east of the villa, a statement of agricultural prowess. Here was a comprehensive building programme meticulously planned and lavishly funded. The temple-mausoleum was a necessary part of the refurbishment for a villa-owner who wanted to make his mark on the landscape, in death as in life. Even in his burial place, he dominated the site, presiding over the buildings below. Just like the circular shrine before it (and several times its size), the temple-mausoleum would have been clearly visible to visitors entering the villa at the east, as it was in direct sightline behind the villa. Its monumentality represented a statement of the owner's sophistication and power, his control of the landscape, and was an expression of piety.

The authors of the GIS study in Bartlow (see Chapter Two 'Landscape setting') argued that barrows are 'active and symbolically charged statements about power and identity' and this could apply equally to Lullingstone's temple-mausoleum. The villa and its temple would have been visible from a long distance from all directions (other than the west where the hillside obscured the view), as they were in a prominent position on terraces rising above the riverbank.[42] However, Eckardt warns of the potential problems with GIS and, in particular viewshed analysis, for example the effect of trees, and even the height of an observer, on visibility.[43] While such a scientific study would be welcome at Lullingstone, these are all limitations that would need to be considered.

Of particular note for our consideration of Lullingstone is Eckardt's conclusion that the barrows' display of power and wealth was directed very much at a local audience.[44] Lullingstone villa (with temple-mausoleum) likewise addressed its local population (including that on the villa estate) and neighbouring élites, namely those residing nearby along the Darent Valley. We shall return to this point in Chapter Three ('An incongruous combination?').

Granary

Between AD 293-297 a large granary was constructed along the north side of the possible garden in front of the house.[45] It was capable of storing a large amount of corn, its dimensions 24.4m long by 10.68 m wide.[46] This indicates the purpose of occupation of the villa at this time was predominantly agricultural.[47] The construction

---

[41] Wilson 2009: 30.
[42] Meates 1963: 3.
[43] Eckardt et al. 2009: 69 and 74.
[44] Eckardt et al. 2009: 76.
[45] Meates 1955: 114.
[46] Meates 1979: 23.
[47] Meates 1955: 109.

Figure 2.14. Granary: view looking north-east. Meates 1979: 207, Plate XXIIIa. © Kent Archaeological Society.

included a raised floor, with small brick arches in the east and west exterior walls. These would allow air to circulate beneath the floor and dry any corn being stored above and prevent it from becoming mouldy. There was also a south corridor where the same aeration seems to have occurred, as another brick arch was built into the exterior wall and rows of piers were built to support the floor [fig. 2.14]. The size of the granary provides a useful comparison for other known granaries. Black compiled a table comparing internal floor area of twenty-five granaries in South England, comprising three main categories: those up to 55.7m^2, of which there are seventeen; those between 55.7m^2 and 186m^2, of which there are just three; and those above 186m^2 of which there are five. Lullingstone falls into the latter category, boasting an internal floor area of 276.5m^2. Three of the other top five are also in the Darent Valley - Darenth, Farningham and Horton Kirby.[48] This local density of large granaries, all dated to the late third/early fourth century, indicates that London was a large consumer and/or exporter of grain and that the Darent villas were exploiting this demand.

The granary would thus allow storage on a commercial scale. Under the floor in the centre of the hall there were two square box-like constructions, with a small channel between them to allow the air to pass through [fig. 2.15]. Meates suggested these would be ideal for winnowing - again, this may indicate commercial use. The corridor may have been where they stacked the prepared corn. A large door located centrally in this corridor would have been ideal for taking corn down to the river for export, being just 20m or so from the riverbank. 1982-86 excavations in the field adjacent to the modern car park revealed three large wooden stakes (with others likely) adjacent

---

[48] Black 1987: 60.

Figure 2.15. Granary: central boxes. Meates 1979: 208, Plate XXIVa. © Kent Archaeological Society.

to the site of the granary.[49] These might represent the remnants of a Roman riverbank revetment ideal for the loading/unloading of corn. That discovery, combined with the size of the building, suggests grain could have been collected as tax from neighbouring farms and stored with the villa's own contribution.

The large granary would have complemented the architecture and positioning of the villa. It was unusual for civilian granaries to have aeration[50] and this probably impressed visitors. They would have entered the villa at the east and passed the granary as they approached, enhancing their anticipation of the grandeur of the villa. The granary was at a right angle to the villa but separated by 20.74 m;[51] thus it was very visible from the eastern outlook of the villa, being adjacent to the riverside garden, whilst not detracting from the view.

A supposition that the Lullingstone estate would have farmed many hundreds of acres[52] can be supported by estimated calculations of the granary's storage capacity. One 'guesstimate' proposes that the combined arable and pastoral land (excavated animal remains included cattle, sheep, pig and fowl) amounted to 1,100-1,700 acres.[53] Ownership of cattle was one of the methods for representing status in Roman Britain[54] and the Lullingstone owner perhaps prided himself on his many fields of livestock.

---

[49] Philp and Chenery 2006: Part II.5.
[50] Meates 1979: 112.
[51] Meates 1979: 23.
[52] Meates 1963: 4.
[53] Fulford 2003: 18.
[54] Hingley 2004: 328.

Figure 2.16. Middle Littleton Tithe Barn, a thirteenth century barn in Evesham, Worcestershire. © National Trust Images/ Robert Morris.

The granary may also exemplify 'the conspicuous display of agricultural production, processing and storage'. Taylor argues convincingly for more detailed studies of entire rural settlements and not just domestic buildings, the latter which attract scholarly analysis due to the existence of their mosaics, hypocausts and baths.[55] Thus, ancillary buildings, despite the effort and cost invested in their construction, are frequently overlooked in our enthusiasm to admire the architecture and decoration of the villas themselves.[56] He champions these 'grand constructions… built to impress' and employs Purcell's phrase the 'romance of storage' to underline his point.[57] The prominent position of the granary within the foreground of Lullingstone villa ensured that, if a visitor was admiring the river view from the villa's eastern veranda, he/she could hardly have missed the imposing granary. More modern comparisons may be the tithe barns used in the Middle Ages as symbols of the power and control exercised by the Church [fig 2.16], or even the processing and storage facilities of modern farms.

Taylor summarises: 'In different ways all of these places created a sense of processional theatre in which the halls and granaries were to the fore'. At Lullingstone, visitors were greeted by a stage set of a grand villa, with the temple-mausoleum an imposing background scene framing the main vista of the villa itself. As visitors proceeded to the entrance at the east they became the audience, the theatrical character of the site created by its terracing of the hillside. The granary was functional, but also symbolic - a manifest display of abundance to all visitors including the owner's tenants coming to pay their rent/taxes. People would have come to the villa for various economic reasons and, as such, were both viewers and victims of status architecture.

Taylor also suggests that British villa-owners adopted the aspirational landscape championed by Roman authors such as Pliny the Younger (*Epistulae* 5.6), where

---

[55] Taylor 2011: 180.
[56] Taylor 2011: 186.
[57] Purcell 1995: 169.

diversity in agriculture and land use were visible from the estate villa. The evidence mentioned above, suggesting that mixed arable and pastoral farming was practised at Lullingstone, would support this. It is perhaps a reflection of the traditionally held view of such 'outbuildings' that, despite its almost complete excavation and wealth of archaeological evidence, the granary was backfilled and remains covered by the visitors' carpark. Our view of villas is conditioned by 19th and 20th century excavators who wanted to emphasise *otium* (a sense of ease and leisure) rather than labour. Resources play a major part in the decision to keep this part of the villa complex hidden, but it would help redress the imbalance of our attention on the villas themselves if this impressive structure could be accessible to visitors today.

Before turning our attention to some comparable villas, it is worth mentioning the political and military backdrop to Lullingstone's reconstruction, including the granary, at the end of the third century. Casey's study of the episode of Carausius and Allectus may provide some answers.[58] In AD 286-7 the military commander Carausius led a revolt against the central administration, seizing control of Britain for himself. Seven years later, he was assassinated by his former ally, Allectus, who held the province for only three years before himself being overthrown when Constantius led an invasion to reclaim Britain for the central empire.[59] The rebuilding at Lullingstone therefore coincided with the end of this period of military and political turmoil, the effects of which would have been keenly felt in nearby *Londinium.* We might ask whether the building programme was initiated by an individual in authority keen to make a statement to the local populace. Casey persuasively argues that some of the prosperity of the agricultural community, reflected in the growth of grand villas in the fourth century, may be due to the redistribution of the assets of Carausius and Allectus' supporters.[60] With this in mind, let us now turn to some of Lullingstone's contemporary villas to examine whether similar patterns of display emerge.

Comparable villas

In the fourth century, southern rural England was heavily populated with villas often located at the centre of farm estates.[61] These affluent villas would have been conspicuous, presiding over the surrounding scenery. Sometimes these villas were evidence of production but also of consumption.[62] Martins equates conspicuous consumption with 'competitive spending'.[63] However, belonging to a wealthy and powerful élite, far from being the norm, they were remarkable even then.

The use of landscape to create immediate impact on visitors was used to similar effect in the villa at Great Witcombe in the Coln Valley [figs. 2.17 and 2.18], which was built into a steep hillside with the main part of the complex highest up ensuring that the most important visitors and household members were, quite literally, placed above

---

[58] Casey 1994.
[59] Casey 1994: 39-42.
[60] Casey 1994: 149.
[61] Scott 2000: 81.
[62] Millett 1990: 97.
[63] Martins 2004: 15.

Figure 2.17. Remains of Great Witcombe Roman Villa, Gloucestershire. © Historic England Archive.

Figure 2.18. Reconstruction drawing of Great Witcombe Roman Villa in the fourth century AD (illustration by Ivan Lapper). © Historic England Archive.

everyone else. A further benefit must have been the commanding views along a short valley towards the Cotswold scarp rather than choosing a more extensive view across the Severn flood plain.[64] Here the drama of the setting (c.f. the theatrical setting at Lullingstone above) may have been more important than the extent of the views. In Hampshire, Thruxton villa is positioned to maximise the commanding views to the south and the west.[65] At Castor, near Peterborough, the villa was constructed on several terraces cut into a steep slope, with retaining walls being built as necessary. It not only benefitted from impressive views over its surrounding landscape but would itself have been a presiding feature of the area, conspicuous from most directions.[66] Again, the use of terracing would have added a dramaturgical feel.

Other methods were employed to make an impact on the landscape: at Bignor, at the end of the third century, a great courtyard with north and south wings was added. The imposing courtyard approach, enhanced by its symmetrical façade, 'would have been an impressive feature of the landscape'.[67] The architects built a villa using more than landscape elements to frame the experience. A combination of dramatic architecture and the theatrical setting ensured maximum impact on visitors. A striking effect could even be achieved by using different coloured roof tiles: at Lullingstone, a combination of red and yellow tiles was employed;[68] at Piddington, Northamptonshire, blue and yellow roof tiles were interspersed, offset by red columns. It is easy to forget the bright colour schemes favoured in the ancient world when examining the monochrome remains.[69]

A further case study: Chedworth

Chedworth villa merits a more detailed discussion in the context of its landscape setting and display of wealth and status. It was constructed in a small steep-sided valley of the river Coln, Gloucestershire.[70] The villa appears to have had more than one dining room[71] and the larger of these, at the east end of the north wing, could have provided impressive views over the valley and the landscape beyond. Further, this wing was on a raised level and the relatively open southern aspect would have afforded the dining room direct sun. Pliny the Younger emphasised the benefits of good views and south-facing aspects (*Epistulae* 2.17). The Chedworth owner seems to have taken a leaf out of Pliny's book.

Visitors to the late fourth century villa would have been struck by its impressive stature in its landscape setting [fig. 2.19]. They would have arrived from the east at the opening and the lowest point of the valley. Towering above them bilaterally were the north and south ranges of the villa, the former built into a terrace on the hillside around 5m above the valley floor. Straight ahead was a steep slope which they would climb to reach the threshold of the outer courtyard, beyond which access

---

[64] Scott 2000: 95.
[65] Henig and Soffe 1993.
[66] Esmonde Cleary 2013: 49.
[67] Black 1983 as cited by Scott 2000: 99.
[68] Meates 1955: 96.
[69] De la Bédoyère 2001: 28.
[70] Esmonde Cleary 2013: 14.
[71] Esmonde Cleary 2013: 39.

Figure 2.19. An illustration showing an aerial view of Chedworth Roman Villa as it was in its peak. © National Trust Images.

was controlled. Above the villa, the sides and end of the valley climbed even higher, wrapping around the villa buildings which faced the visitor.[72] It must have been a daunting, if impressive, approach, with different effects on different visitors: the villa-owner would wish to impress his superiors; for his social peers, the villa was a competitive display of wealth and status; to his subordinates, however, this was an undiluted reminder of their lowly status and could have been an intimidating experience, especially imagining if, as at Lullingstone, they were arriving to bring rent or the product of paid or compelled agricultural labour.

Like Lullingstone, the early villa had been constructed on a relatively level (and restricted) terrain but subsequent development of the villa demanded solutions to the problematic slopes. The architects turned this obstacle into an opportunity and utilised the landscape to present the villa in dramatic style, taking centre stage in the backdrop of a theatrical panorama. On the north range, they created an artificial terrace by cutting back into the hillside and further enhanced the level by constructing a platform protruding over the lower part of the valley. The result was a steep, possibly even vertical, precipice rising from the outer courtyard. This was in sharp contrast to the buildings at the eastern part of the south range (possibly the service wing) that were at the lower level and to which access could easily be gained from the outer courtyard. Only the most élite guests would be allowed access through the gate house to the most elevated (in every sense) part of the villa. We are about to see in Chapter Three another example of differentiation between visitors - for this, we shall return to Lullingstone.

---

[72] Esmonde Cleary 2013: 46-7.

Chapter Three

The choice and use of mosaics in the fourth century villa: how the patron presented his cultural identity and status through pavements

Grand designs

In Chapter Two, we examined the landscape setting of the villa and how topography was used to display the owner's wealth and status. We considered the theatrical aspects of the use of terracing, large granary and ostentatious temple-mausoleum. In this chapter, we shall look at the interior of the villa and the added drama provided by the decoration, namely the fourth century mosaics. We shall continue our examination of the owner's theatrical display of wealth and status and shall therefore concentrate on these aspects of the mosaics' themes and their impact on visitors.

From around AD 300, prosperity in Roman Britain enabled a significant increase in villa construction and lavish decoration which lasted through most of the fourth century.[1] Scott provides a useful overview of the changing architecture in fourth century Roman Britain[2] and concludes that a common feature is an increase in dining and reception rooms, combined with elaborate mosaics. The use of mosaics to adorn floors was an enduring expression of the owner's tastes and aspirations. Given we have very little written evidence of civilian life in Roman Britain, these mosaics provide many useful indicators of their social context[3] including the villa-owners' interests, beliefs and wealth (mosaics were expensive luxury goods).[4]

Lullingstone also enjoyed additions and embellishments to its reception rooms in the fourth century [see p. vi, 'Villa plan'] and, as first examined by Wallace-Hadrill for houses in other parts of the empire,[5] the layout of the house was created to meet the needs of the owner and a wide variety of visitors.[6] The terms 'private' and 'public', which we might use when describing houses and buildings today, cannot be applied in the same way to Roman villas.[7] Whilst the villa-owners had space, they shared it with a large group of others. At Lullingstone, given the construction of the large granary in AD 293-7[8] and the implied success of the estate as a thriving agricultural enterprise, visitors to the villa would have included tenants and farmworkers as well as the patron's social peers from the Darent Valley and beyond. Thus, we cannot look at Lullingstone as having completely distinct agricultural and residential parts. Estate-

---

[1] Barrett 1978: 307. Dunbabin 1999: 91. Prosperity was partly a result of exploitation: Millett 1990.
[2] Scott 2000: 77-112.
[3] Ling 1997: 280.
[4] Scott 2000: 169.
[5] Wallace Hadrill: 1988. (Mainly of earlier periods.)
[6] Ellis 1995: 163.
[7] Dunbabin 1994: 171.
[8] Meates 1955: 114.

workers, tenants and other clients would not have been confined exclusively to either part. However, their movement around the villa would have been carefully controlled by the architecture and décor. We shall therefore put into practice a Wallace-Hadrill style approach by tracing their steps as they entered the villa from the east.

The central room

The central room was a part of the villa which had been in use in every phase of its occupation but in c. AD 330-60[9] it was given a facelift with the instalment of a lavish mosaic [fig. 3.1]. This mosaic was directly ahead when visitors arrived via the main eastern entrance. Having climbed the wooden staircase, visitors would cross the veranda which ran along the east side of the villa and reach the central room measuring 4.8m by 6.25m.[10] Visitors would have first stepped onto a border of plain red tesserae, probably a walkway as it was laid on three sides of the room with an elaborate mosaic within. Nearest the entrance, but orientated at 180 degrees from it, was Bellerophon mounted on the winged horse Pegasus and killing the Chimaera. Surrounded by a cushion shaped guilloche, this part of the mosaic also contained four dolphins and two shell-type objects. Around the guilloche was a plain, square border, the four corners of which each contained a roundel depicting one of the four seasons, represented by female busts. Between the Bellerophon panel and the apse was a rectangular chequerboard mosaic, made up of 55 sections of various designs including hearts, swastikas and petals.[11] The symbols could have apotropaic purposes, complementing the seasons' symbols of prosperity. This chequerboard and the Bellerophon panel are bordered on the north, east and south sides by a repeating pattern of a swastika.

The location and size of this room suggest that it served as an audience chamber, like the *atrium* in Italian villas, where the aristocrat held his morning *salutatio* (greeting) by his clients. The British equivalent might have been the farmworkers coming to the villa to receive instructions for the day, or tenants coming to pay their rent.[12] At Lullingstone, the central room would be of sufficient size and had easy access from the main entrance whilst also reflecting the superior social status of the owner of the estate. As well as the interior décor, the position of the room lent import to the occasion of visits here. Facing the veranda with its open colonnade, the view from this room included the garden, the river and the countryside beyond. The value of such views to the Roman élite is evident in literature (Pliny the Younger: *Epistulae* 5.6.14-20 and Sidonius Apollinaris: *Epistulae* 2.2.10-14) and wall-painting.[13] As seen in Chapter Two, 'a room with a view' is not just a modern taste but one which was appreciated in Roman times, too.

---

[9] Meates 1979: 84.
[10] Measurements after Meates 1951: 44.
[11] Meates 1979: 79 and 82-3.
[12] Ellis 1995: 166.
[13] Bergmann 1991: 49-70.

Figure 3.1. Detail: Bellerophon on Pegasus, spearing the Chimaera. c. AD 330-60. © Historic England Archive.

The seasons

At the entrance to the central room, excavations revealed post-holes and wooden uprights which would have enabled heavy curtains to be hung, providing the owner with the option of restricting access.[14] Meates recorded the absence of iron hinges, concluding doors were not hung here. The excavators also found evidence of the floor having been repaired to the south-east border which suggests that this bore the most traffic and may be where visitors entered. It also suggests they moved in a clockwise direction.[15] Bellerophon would be upside down as they entered but, as they moved around the room, he would come into direct view. What they would be facing on arrival (and had time to contemplate as they awaited access) were the two seasons on the west side.

---

[14] Meates 179: 84.

[15] Meates 1955: 30.

Figure 3.2. Detail: Summer. c. AD 330-60. © Historic England Archive.

The south-west season is now missing so its attributes are unknown; the north-west one has corn-stalks in her hair [fig. 3.2]. Usually corn is thought to represent Summer (as at Rudston and Brading [fig. 3.4])[16] but here, this would mean the normal, clockwise rotation[17] of the seasons through Spring, Summer, Autumn, Winter would not work as Autumn and Summer would have been swapped. If the missing season was indeed Autumn, it is likely to have had an attribute such as a rake, representing rural activities at harvest.[18] Putting aside the question about 'correct' order, of more significance might be that the images of corn and the (assumed) rake would be the first two depictions that would face the visitor as he entered. As this mosaic was installed at the height of the estate's agricultural success (c.f. the granary construction), such deliberate placing of these two seasons (with harvest-related attributes) reinforced and celebrated the agricultural efficiency and wealth of this farm. It was a visual representation of the prosperity brought by the Darent Valley's natural resources combined with the farmworkers' toiling. These farmworkers would congregate by these mosaics each day and be reminded of their patron's success. Other visitors would include neighbouring landowners who might measure their own success against Lullingstone.

Seasons were a popular mosaic choice in Roman Britain (c.f. Brading [figs. 3.3, 3.4 and 3.5] and Littlecote) and the rest of empire: at Ravenna in Italy, like Lullingstone,

---

[16] Ling 1983: 16-18.

[17] Ling presents persuasive arguments for clockwise being the usual rotation 1983: 18.

[18] Ling 1983: 20.

Figure 3.3. Brading Roman Villa mosaic: Spring. © Oglander Roman Trust.

Figure 3.4. Brading Roman Villa mosaic: Summer. © Oglander Roman Trust.

Figure 3.5. Brading Roman Villa mosaic: Winter. © Oglander Roman Trust.

they appeared with Bellerophon and the Chimaera.[19] Their convenient fit for four corners of a quadrangular design helps explain their recurrence,[20] but they carried a more meaningful message, too. There is a logical order to presenting the year as passing through its natural course; a reference perhaps to the owner's control of the landscape around him (c.f. Chapter Two). The swastika (in the meandering border) was a solar symbol, which here also reinforced the pattern of movement prompted by the seasons' configuration. Seasons have also been interpreted as reflecting the liberality of the owner[21], the abundance of nature translating into the munificence of a generous host particularly one who farmed the land, and this might be exactly the message the Lullingstone patron had in mind, at a time when he was investing finances in his property.

Bellerophon

First impressions were therefore being carefully managed and the theme of Bellerophon and the Chimaera was also a deliberate choice. This was a motif also chosen at Croughton in Northamptonshire, Frampton, and Hinton St Mary [fig. 3.6].[22] As recently as 2017, a community archaeology project revealed another Bellerophon mosaic at Mud Hole villa in Boxford, Berkshire, dated mid/late fourth century.[23] Like Lullingstone, this villa had been terraced into the hillside achieving a similar theatrical setting. The excavations revealed fragmentary inscriptions of Bellerophon's name and possibly that of King Proetus (also depicted) who, according to mythology, banished Bellerophon. This implies viewers would have known the story.

Bellerophon's story included adventures similar to those of Heracles. While a guest of King Proetus in Argos, Bellerophon rejected the Queen's advances. Furious at his rejection, the Queen denounced him and Bellerophon was sent by the King to the Queen's father bearing a sealed letter demanding the young man's death. Consequently, Bellerophon was set dangerous tasks likely to kill him including destroying the fire-breathing Chimaera. This was a monster comprising a lion's head, a goat's body and a serpent for a tail. Against the odds, Bellerophon successfully completed the tasks with the help of his winged horse Pegasus.

Bellerophon could represent a heroic model for the patron's own hunting exploits[24] by depicting a skilled horseman conquering a wild and treacherous beast. The hero could even allude to the political power and influence of the villa-owner.[25] It was a popular scene in Roman Britain,[26] comprehensible to most viewers familiar with Homer's *Iliad* in which the story was first told (6.155-202). The Homeric reference therefore reflects Lullingstone's owner's classical learning, a message consistently conveyed in all the mosaics he chose. Bellerophon has also been interpreted as representing the triumph

---

[19] Ellis 1995: 175.
[20] Ling 1983: 19. Ling 1997: 275.
[21] Ellis 1995: 175.
[22] Ling 1997: 262-3 and 274.
[23] Beeson: 2018.
[24] Ling 1997: 278-9.
[25] Ellis 1995: 175.
[26] Beeson 2018: 89.

Figure 3.6. Detail of Pegasus and the Chimaera, Hinton St Mary. Early fourth century AD. © 2019 The Trustees of the British Museum.

of death over evil[27] and could therefore support religious interpretations of the mosaics, which are well-documented in scholarship.[28] Whether a religious allusion was inferred or not, the triumphant scene of Bellerophon would have announced to visitors that they were entering the home of a successful landowner. Combined with the seasons and the liberality they suggested, expectations of the sort of hospitality his élite visitors might enjoy would be high. One way of demonstrating his generosity would be to throw lavish dinner parties, or *convivia*. The audience chamber by day would transform into an impressive reception room by night - the perfect setting for mingling before moving to the *triclinium* for *cena*. The radial positioning of the season

---

[27] Toynbee 1964: 264-5.
[28] See e.g. Perring: 2003.

Figure 3.7. Tombstone of Julia Velva depicting apsidal dining room, AD 200-300. (YORYM: 1998.25). © York Museums Trust (Yorkshire Museum).

images probably encouraged circulation, with the mosaics as a conversation piece.[29] Only the élite would be invited to partake in *convivia*, the highlight of which would take place in the apse, to which we shall now move.

The apse

In the late third century, provincial Roman houses started to include an apsidal *triclinium*, a feature of Italian houses (and, exceptionally in Britain, Fishbourne) from the first century AD [fig. 3.7]. The apse was an appropriate shape for a semi-circular couch (*stibadium*) on which diners would recline, a development from the earlier U-shape arrangement of three couches, hence *triclinium* as the usual name for Roman dining-rooms. In the first century, Martial wrote that his *stibadium* could accommodate seven or eight diners (*Epigrams* 10.18.6; 14.8.7).[30] *Stibadia* allowed for the social ranking of guests, with the most important diner taking the right end of the couch [fig. 3.8].

[29] Witts 2000: 316-318.
[30] Cosh 2001: 226.

The apsidal room at Lullingstone was added as part of the overall embellishment of the villa c. AD 330-60[31] when, as noted above, Roman Britain was enjoying a period of prosperity.[32] It reflected a trend of apsidal rooms with mosaics in contemporary Romano-British villas including Bignor, Dewlish, Hinton St Mary, Frampton and, on a larger scale, Littlecote, which boasted a multi-apsed dining-room.[33] The apse at Lullingstone was the 'architectural climax' to the villa,[34] with a 23cm high step leading from the audience chamber to the apse's entrance, providing a natural extension to the space used for receiving clients and entertaining guests [figs. 3.9 and 3.10].[35] At 6.25m wide and 4.88m deep, it formed a horseshoe shape with a plain border varying in width from 2m to over 3m. Within it was a figured panel, also horseshoe shaped

Figure 3.8. Reconstruction of Lullingstone's apsidal dining room with *stibadium*. c. AD 330-60 (illustration by Peter Dunn). © Historic England Archive.

[31] Meates 1979: 73.
[32] Leader-Newby 2007: 190-3.
[33] Ellis 1995: 171 and 176. Scott 2000: 92-101.
[34] Scott 2004: 48.
[35] Barrett 1978: 310.

Figure 3.9. View across central audience chamber to apse with step (looking south). Meates 1979: 201, Plate XVIIb. © Kent Archaeological Society.

Figure 3.10. View across central audience chamber to apse with step (looking north west). Meates 1979: 201, Plate XVIIc. © Kent Archaeological Society.

with a width of 2.44m and a maximum length of 2.44m.[36] An analysis by Ellis[37] of sixteen contemporary apsidal dining rooms shows Lullingstone's to be of average size. Given the villa was not particularly large, this suggests the proportion of reception areas to the rest of the villa is what we would expect.

---

[36] Measurements after Meates 1951: 44.

[37] Ellis 1995: 177, Table 1.

The figure scene in the apse portrays Europa riding on a bull over the sea, accompanied by two cupids with an inscription above. Before considering the image and inscription, let us consider the architectural setting [fig. 3.11]. The part of the apse hidden by the *stibadium* was usually deliberately left plain[38] and at Lullingstone the horseshoe shaped area around the central picture is in plain red terracotta tesserae. This strongly indicates the room was used for dining and it was likely also used as an extension of the audience chamber.[39] The *stibadium* was a moveable piece of furniture (as was the low table on which dinner would be served), so the room could easily be adapted to suit the occasion.

The shape of the apse provided an obvious focal point and thus the architecture lent itself to the function of an audience hall in which the *dominus* sat in the apse to receive his visitors who would proceed through the central room, perhaps in an orderly queue awaiting their turn to be received. The theatricality of such a procession allowed the *dominus* to act out his role, and at Lullingstone the apse's elevation above the step (itself decorated with a mosaic) created a perfect stage. Such an architectural setting 'allowed aristocrats to emulate the solemnity and separateness of the emperors'.[40] Whether Romano-British élites were consciously modelling themselves on the emperor or simply copying the custom of the Roman élite (who themselves were

Figure 3.11. Reconstruction of Lullingstone's audience chamber and apse. c. AD 330-60 (illustration by Peter Dunn). © Historic England Archive.

[38] Ellis 1995: 171. Ling 1998: 118.
[39] Neal 1991: 13-15. Witts 2000: 299.
[40] Scott 2004: 52.

imitating the emperor's practice), this behaviour and the architecture in which it was played out was reflected in provincial villas, including Lullingstone. The apse became a backdrop, a stage-set on which the owner assumed the leading role[41] either when delivering morning instructions to his farmworkers or taking centre stage for the *convivium,* itself a performance for an invited audience.

If we apply Wallace-Hadrill's approach[42] to Lullingstone, we can see how differentials between classes of visitors could be indicated by access to different rooms. The apsidal *triclinium* does not open straight off the veranda where the main entrance was located and thus it was not easily accessible for all comers. Access to the apse was controlled,[43] with visitors having to negotiate their way through the audience chamber first. Access to the *triclinium* was by invitation only, according to Vitruvius (*De Architectura* 6.5.1).[44] Should any farmworkers be tempted to proceed further than they should, the step provided a physical barrier. If the *dominus* chose to sit in the apse and address them from there, the orientation of the mosaic within that space (facing the back of the apse and therefore away from anyone confined to the audience chamber) would have magnified his superiority, as only he could view the mosaic from the correct viewpoint.[45]

Europa and the bull

With so many opportunities to display his tastes and showcase his culture, the owner will have thought carefully about what to depict on the stage where he would regularly perform. Here, his leading lady is Europa [fig. 3.12]. Depicted riding on the back of a bull (Jupiter in disguise) who bounds over the sea, she is naked but for a diaphanous garment one end of which covers her lower half, the other which billows out behind her suggesting a breeze. Her raised right hand holds her robe behind her, with her left hand she holds onto the bull's neck. She wears two armlets, a bracelet and a necklace. One cupid leads the way, holding a torch in one hand, the other raised up in encouragement. A second follows behind and appears to be pulling the bull back by his tail [fig. 3.13]. Whether he is indeed attempting to restrain the bull (and his erotic desire)[46] or this is simply 'playful sport',[47] the pair of cupids provides symmetry to the image and adds a spirited and light-hearted ambience.

The Europa image does not seem to be a standard pattern-book design, which suggests it was a special commission for the Lullingstone patron.[48] Only one other example of this story in mosaic has been found in Roman Britain, at Keynsham, Somerset in a hexagonal multi-apsed dining-room opening on the great courtyard of the villa [fig. 3.14].[49] It depicts an earlier stage of Jupiter's abduction, before he whisked her off

---

[41] Scott 2000: 107-8.
[42] Wallace Hadrill 1998.
[43] Witts 2000: 321
[44] Witts 2000: 312.
[45] Witts 2000: 321.
[46] Meates 1955: 38.
[47] Barrett 1978: 310.
[48] Leader-Newby 2007: 192.
[49] Ellis 1995: 175-6.

Figure 3.12. Europa mosaic. c. AD 330-60. © Historic England Archive.

over the sea. The bull is resting on the beach, while seated Europa decorates him with garlands and her companion offers the bull a basket of flowers.[50] This is a more tranquil scene than the vivacious and playful nature of the Lullingstone mosaic, perhaps designed more for its aesthetic qualities than as a talking point. It is one of a group of mosaics which indicate the owner wanted to create a collection of Graeco-Roman emblemata.[51] The Lullingstone patron's motives were similar but, by choosing one main myth in the apse, he can make a more deliberate point beyond his general Classical learning.

Figure 3.13. Detail: Cupid. c. AD 330-60. © Historic England Archive.

---

[50] Barrett 1978: 310. Stupperich 1980: 293.
[51] Stupperich 1980: 296.

Figure 3.14. Europa mosaic. Keynsham. Fourth century AD.
© www.bathnewseum.com

The inscription

As if the Classical image of Europa and the bull did not do justice to his *paideia*, the patron decided to go one step further and distinguished his creation by superimposing an inscription:

INVIDA SI TA[URI] VIDISSET IUNO NATATUS
IUSTIUS AEOLIAS ISSET ADUSQUE DOMOS

If jealous Juno had seen the swimming of the bull,
more justly would she have gone to the halls of Aeolus.[52]

The allusion is to Book 1 (50) of Virgil's *Aeneid* where Juno visits Aeolus (god of the winds), asking him to send a storm to blow the Trojan, Aeneas, off course and prevent him reaching Italy and thus fulfilling his destiny. Juno opposes the Trojans because (*inter alia*) their founder was Dardanus, the illegitimate offspring of Juno's husband Jupiter and his lover Electra. This extra-marital affair explains Juno's jealousy and anger at her husband's support of the Trojans, hence her visit to Aeolus. Jupiter's infidelity, however, was a recurring theme in mythology and Ovid's *Metamorphoses* 2.846-75 recounts Jupiter's transformation into a bull to trick and seduce Europa. The

---

[52] Author's translation.

inscription, therefore, intimates that, had Juno known about this further infidelity, she would have had additional reason to wish destruction on her husband's protégé, Aeneas, and thus even more justification for her trip to Aeolus.[53]

The reference to the *Aeneid* seemed obvious to those who discovered the mosaic.[54] Barrett, however, detected a second literary allusion - the inscription is not written in the hexameters of the *Aeneid*, but as an elegiac couplet, the metre favoured by Ovid. Moreover, Ovid often employed mythology didactically, usually as a conditional sentence, to make a point.[55] Barrett concluded that the inscription's linguistic style together with 'its lighthearted erotic flavour' was a clear reference to Ovid as well as Virgil. This combination of two literary traditions has been widely accepted ever since.[56] Cosh has recently proposed that it is also a parody of a poem by Martial on the same subject.[57]

Scholars also agree the lines were written specifically for this mosaic; the inscription derives meaning from the image and would be harder to comprehend without it. Yet this relationship works both ways as the elegiac couplet also influences the interpretation of the episode depicted. Given the meter, it was probably intended to be read aloud, and we can imagine the patron (possibly the author of the lines) reciting it to impress his guests. Equally, as guests filtered into the apse in anticipation of their *convivium*, it would have been a lively conversation piece. Measuring 0.3m deep and orientated towards the rear of the apse, it could easily be read by diners as they reclined on the *stibadium*, so the discussion could continue over *cena*. That it was intended to be viewed from this angle is demonstrated by the mosaicist's attempt at perspective - when observed directly from above, Europa's body appears elongated but from the *stibadium's* viewpoint, she assumes perfect proportions.[58] The inscription alters the usual viewpoint of the story from the two protagonists, Jupiter and Europa, and introduces a third character, Juno. Juno's perspective as the onlooker is mirrored by the patron and his guests who are also invited to observe the adulterous scene and react.[59] The mosaic also plays, like other interior decoration (such as that at Pompeii), with references to behaviour subverting social norms. Depictions of extra-marital escapades or non-heroic behaviour exemplify the antithesis of the decorum expected of a *paterfamilias* and could be the host's way of cracking a joke at his own expense.

If the elegiac couplet was the patron's own composition, it reflects an education based on that of the Roman élite, with Virgil and Ovid on the syllabus. Such cultural and literary knowledge would be shared with his peers also educated by a *grammaticus* and then *rhetor,* and these social equals would be among the invitees to the patron's *convivia*. Kruschwitz describes this appropriation of high literature as 'impression

---

[53] Henig 1995: 157-8, Kruschwitz 2015: 54 and Perring 2003: 117.
[54] Meates 1979: 77.
[55] Barrett 1978: 311-2.
[56] Elsner 1998: 137. Henig 1995: 157-8. Leader-Newby 2007: 190-3.
[57] Cosh 2016.
[58] Barrett 1978: 310. Meates 1955: 40-1.
[59] Kruschwitz 2015: 54.

management... to an extreme'.⁶⁰ Literary sources reveal the villas were both 'points of contact and entertainment between aristocrats, and also centres of display'.⁶¹ Sidonius praises Consentius and his villa as a setting for the flow of 'swift iambics, pointed elegiacs, rounded hendecasyllables, and all the other verses fragrant with thyme and flowers...' (*Epistulae*. 8.4 c. AD 478). The Lullingstone patron may have been ahead of his time, given he included an elegiac couplet in his villa's decoration over a century earlier than Sidonius' reference.

A controversial paper in 1997 claimed the inscription had hidden Christian meanings. By a complex numerical formula, Henig advocated that the name 'Jesus' was contained within the words, only to be seen by those who knew to look for it. Although he has received some support/acknowledgment for this theory,⁶² others have dismissed his conclusion as only being reached in a 'needlessly convoluted and cryptic manner'.⁶³ Instead, Kruschwitz argues the Europa image and its inscription are firmly based in the tradition of pagan Classical literature and mythology. As with Bellerophon, the overriding message that the owner wanted to convey was his *paideia*, his wealth and, by the inscription, his wit.

There are few examples in Britain of inscriptions identifying figures in mosaics: Lullingstone is exceptional, as were inscriptions found at Frampton and Thruxton.⁶⁴ Patrons therefore usually anticipated that their guests had a reasonable acquaintance with mythology and its traditional iconography or were content that the visual effect of the images was sufficient to impress. In other parts of the empire, inscriptions at the threshold of dining rooms were more common.⁶⁵ At the palace of Theodoric at Ravenna (mentioned at 'The seasons', above), the seasons mosaic of its triconch dining room was accompanied by an inscription referring to the fertility of the harvest and the generosity of the host.⁶⁶ The inscription was therefore an integral part of the composition, and the propaganda advertising the host's intellectual prowess and generosity.

At a villa in Contigny, Lausanne (AD 60-80/90) the graffiti of a pupil learning Greek is regarded as evidence of the cultural aspirations of the villa-owner's family. Particularly famous for being a palindrome, it is written in a meter very similar to the dactylic hexameter of Homer's *Iliad* and *Odyssey*. Both Latin and Greek formed part of a classical education.⁶⁷ Similarly, in Pompeii, Rome and the villa of Ahrweiler, Germany, pupils scribbled on walls with verses of Virgil or Ovid. Graffiti represents a fleeting moment, a spontaneous wish to express oneself in everyday life,⁶⁸ whereas at Lullingstone the mosaic's inscription involved a more permanent method. However,

---

⁶⁰ Kruschwitz 2015: 3.
⁶¹ Scott 2004: 43.
⁶² Henig 1997: 4-7. Neal and Cosh 2009: 385.
⁶³ Kruschwitz 2015: 54. See also Ling 1997: 279-80 who is reluctant to accept hidden meanings.
⁶⁴ Stupperich 1980: 298-301.
⁶⁵ Ellis 1995: 171.
⁶⁶ Ellis 1991: 125-6.
⁶⁷ Fuchs and Dubois 1997: 182.
⁶⁸ Fuchs and Dubois 1997: 183.

the sentiment behind its conception stems from a similar desire to put one's own mark on a building. The Lullingstone owner's parading of his linguistic skills in an Ovidian elegiac couplet reveals a spirit similar to that in some ancient Classical graffiti from Switzerland and France, which included plays on words and language games.[69]

Perhaps more closely aligned to the Lullingstone example is a mosaic discovered in Provence, which appropriated some lines from Martial.[70] The epigram accompanied a fifth century mosaic depicting Bacchus and the Three Graces and again draws in the viewer by inviting him to observe and react to the images. The combination of Classical imagery and poetry is an ostensible display of the owner's cultural learning and a springboard for intellectual conversation with his guests.

An incongruous combination?

We have seen above the repeated theme of the Lullingstone owner wishing to impress by conveying his erudite background. His choice of mosaics and their juxtaposition with the Latin couplet demonstrate a fondness for Classical mythology and literature but also 'a sophisticated familiarity' with it.[71] The inscription is a striking example of late antique *paideia*. However, some scholars have questioned whether the 'high classicism' of the couplet is at odds with the provincial and schematic style of the images.[72]

The schematic style derives from the figures being outlined in red tesserae with only Europa's garment, hair, and the cupids' hair and wings blocked with colour, creating a one-dimensional effect. Similarly, Dunbabin differentiates between the main figure of Bellerophon - 'skilfully and clearly drawn' - and 'the incompetent design of some of the lesser parts'. The dolphins have some curious features, such as their slug-like bodies,[73] suggesting the artist was unfamiliar with their anatomy. Perhaps several different mosaicists completed the mosaic, with the main part worked on by an itinerant extra-provincial mosaicist and the minor parts delegated to local, lesser skilled craftsmen.[74]

On the other hand, Scott warns of the dangers of making 'unfavourable aesthetic judgments about those artforms which we deem to be less technically and aesthetically competent when viewed at a provincial or empire-wide level.'[75] As she points out, the patron, the mosaicist and the viewer may only have local experience of such art; it is misguided therefore for us to judge the aesthetic or intellectual effect based on our own knowledge. Scott also emphasises the 'social position of the interpreter'. Thus, at Lullingstone, as well as the educated invitees to the *triclinium*, we should remember that the mosaics in the audience chamber will have been seen by workers and tenants who did not benefit from a Classical education but who may have admired the images at a more superficial level. This was not the audience at which the high Classical

[69] Barbet and Fuchs 2008: 167-72.
[70] Lavagne 2000: 315-20.
[71] Bowden and Pearce 2017: 23.
[72] Elsner 1998: 136-8. Leader-Newby 2007: 190-3.
[73] Henig 1997: 4.
[74] Dunbabin 1999: 98.
[75] Scott 2000: 16. See also comments re the local audience in Chapter Two 'Circular shrine and temple-mausoleum'.

Figure 3.15. Otford wall-painting and inscription. Early second century AD. © 2019 The Trustees of the British Museum.

allusions were aimed: they would not have been expected to engage intellectually with them in the same way as the invitees to the apse. Nevertheless, even if the lavish mosaics simply impressed upon them the spending-power of their patron, his superior status was successfully communicated.

Classical literature in other Romano-British villas

A long-term provincial tradition of Virgil for didactic purposes is demonstrated by the Vindolanda writing tablets from Hadrian's Wall (c. AD 85-130) on which lines from Virgil's *Georgics* were used for writing practice.[76] There were even recherché allusions to Virgil's *Eclogues* on Carausius' coinage.[77] Further evidence of Virgil forming part of education for the élite in Roman Britain[78] was discovered in 1926 just a few miles from Lullingstone, at Progress Villa in Otford where an early second century wall-painting included a scene from the Aeneid together with an inscription [fig. 3.15]. We do not know the owner's identity[79] but he clearly wished to display his cultural learning. Only part of the inscription survived: 'BINA MANU L' which formed the start of a line occurring twice in the *Aeneid* (1.313 and 12.165):

bina manu lato crispans hastalia ferro

brandishing in his hand two broad-bladed spears.[80]

---

[76] Bowman et al. 2010.
[77] Bowden and Pearce 2017: 24.
[78] Dunbabin 1999: 96-7. Henig 1995: 126.
[79] Henig 1995: 69.
[80] Author's translation.

The fragment of wall-painting depicts the arm and body of a man brandishing a spear (the second spear possibly missing), with flesh tones on a dark background. Just as with Lullingstone, the inscription lends meaning to the image.[81] As this was not a particularly frequently cited line,[82] the viewer would need to have good knowledge of the *Aeneid* to recognise the reference. The line could have been chosen by the owner from his own library, with an illustrated scroll inspiring both the inscription and the accompanying figure scene.[83] It is highly likely that there were scribes and illuminators working in Roman Britain who could have created copies of such books for the aristocracy.[84]

In Barrett's assessment of knowledge of the literary Classics in Roman Britain, he also considers a fourth century mosaic from Low Ham, Somerset.[85] Paving the floor of the *frigidarium* in the baths, the mosaic comprises five panels each depicting an episode from the story of Dido and Aeneas, the scenes based closely on *Aeneid* Books 1 and 4 [fig. 3.16]. Whilst it therefore suggests detailed knowledge of Virgil by the owner, the evidence for a personal affinity with the subject chosen is not as compelling as at Lullingstone, where the inscribed image has all the marks of a deliberate choice that was made to measure for its setting. By contrast, the Low Ham images have been squeezed into a tight space - the surrounding walls were within inches of the images so viewers could not stand outside the mosaic to appreciate it, which the images demand. The priority seems to have been visual impact,[86] suggesting a design from a copy book.[87] That said, if the owner knew his Virgil and could assume a similar knowledge on the part of his guests, he might have commissioned a design that did not fit the dimensions perfectly but which made up for any such 'inadequacy' by its narrative qualities.

All these villas present persuasive evidence of owners aspiring to the lifestyle of the aristocracy who ran the Empire's central administration. This included architectural elements and social behaviour. The kind of lifestyle which they were trying to emulate is portrayed in the letters of Sidonius Apollinaris who describes various activities with his neighbours including hunting, dinner parties, correspondence and exchanges of agricultural produce.[88] All these are represented at Lullingstone: Bellerophon, the apsidal dining room, the elegiac couplet and the showpiece granary. These elements certainly make sense in the context of a villa near London, through which passed many figures from this 'central administration'.

---

[81] Kruschwitz 2015: 59.
[82] Barrett 1978: 309.
[83] Henig 1995: 119.
[84] Henig 1995: 157-8.
[85] Barrett 1978:
[86] Barrett 1978: 309.
[87] Toynbee 1964: 246 proposes a North African origin due to connections with Dido's home, Carthage.
[88] Ellis 1995: 164.

The choice and use of mosaics in the fourth century villa

Figure 3.16. Scenes from Virgil's Aeneid. Low Ham mosaic, fourth century AD. © Somerset Archaeological and Natural History Society and South West Heritage Trust, 2019.

Chapter Four

Additional reconstructions of the villa

Illustrations are a wonderful way to bring the remains of a Roman Villa to life and this chapter is therefore included to showcase some new reconstructions, which are here being published in print for the first time.

The images are intended to provide an impression of what Lullingstone Roman Villa might have looked like during the period which is discussed throughout this book, namely the late third and fourth centuries AD. Following the order of the preceding chapters, the first set of images illustrate the villa in its landscape setting; the second set of images showcase the imagined interior decoration, specifically following the lavish embellishments which the owner commissioned in c. AD 330-360.

A certain amount of artistic licence has been applied in the creation of these models. Where an assumption about a particular detail has been made, or a choice based on a number of possible variants (for example, from archaeological evidence elsewhere in the Roman empire), the notes accompanying each image refer to these where possible. In other words, these images should not be interpreted as strict historical records. Instead, their inclusion here aims to assist our understanding and vision of Lullingstone Roman Villa holistically, including the architectural proportions within the surrounding topography, the meticulously planned interior space and, above all, its function and role as an individual's home. In order to emphasise the domestic aspects of the villa, these images do not include any of the ancillary buildings discussed in Chapter Two.

The villa within its landscape setting

These 3D images were created by Rob Sherratt and are reproduced here with his kind permission. Figure 4.1. shows the impressive façade of the villa which would have greeted visitors on arrival (and indeed anyone passing by in a boat on the River Darent). The front garden rises gently upwards from the riverbank towards the east wing of the villa. Behind the villa, the steeply rising slope encompassed the terracing which was created to build the circular shrine and subsequently the temple-mausoleum (see Chapter Two). Neither of those are shown in this reconstruction but we can imagine them being visible behind the villa, even from this view, thanks to their raised foundations and carefully designed roofs which ensured the buildings made their mark on the landscape.

An alternative view (Figure 4.2.) is from the granary, which was positioned to the north-east of the villa, alongside the formal garden (for which evidence is explained on page 12) and close to the west bank of the River Darent. This angle demonstrates well the grandeur of the villa - the roof tiles were a mix of red and yellow for added dramatic effect (see page 22). On the right-hand side of Figure 4.2. is the house-church and at the far right is the door where worshippers would have entered, without having to intrude on the approach to the main front entrance reserved for other visitors.

Additional reconstructions of the villa 45

Figure 4.1. View of Lullingstone Roman Villa from south-east. (3D Reconstruction with Modo Software.) © Rob Sherratt.

Figure 4.2. View of Lullingstone Roman Villa from north-east. (3D Reconstruction with Modo Software.) © Rob Sherratt.

Figure 4.3. View of Lullingstone Roman Villa from south-west. (3D Reconstruction with Modo Software.) © Rob Sherratt.

The rear view of the villa (Figure 4.3.) shows the exterior architecture of the fashionable apsidal dining room at the centre. This image also gives a perspective of the hillside into which the villa was constructed, ensuring sweeping views down to the River Darent and the fields beyond. The perceived value of such an idyllic rural setting is in keeping with what we know from Roman authors about the aesthetics of a desirable home (see page 13).

The villa's interior space and decoration

All the remaining images in this chapter are photographs of a model which was created by Rod Shelton and are reproduced here with his kind permission. The model is currently on display at Lullingstone Castle.

The complete model (Figure 4.4.) shows the extent of the multi-functional living space which included the main reception rooms in the centre of the villa, the bath complex at the south (shown on the left in this image), and the house church at the north (on the right in this image). As discussed in Chapter Three, the owner of Lullingstone would have restricted and carefully choreographed the movements of visitors around this internal space. The pergola in the room adjacent to the central room is consistent with Meates' interpretation that this was an open courtyard. However, subsequent excavations by Dr David Neal suggested that there was not in fact an open courtyard within the villa.[1] This detail of the model, though, reminds us the owners may have created a formal garden in front of the villa (see below).

Figure 4.5. imagines how the inhabitants and their guests would have entered and exited the main part of the villa. The couple shown are descending from the veranda and would be stepping down into what is likely to have been a formal garden, between the villa and the River Darent (see page 12). As they were leaving the villa, they would have enjoyed an impressive view across the river to the fields beyond, of which Pliny might have approved (see page 19).

---

[1] Wilson 2009:40.

Figure 4.4. The floorplan of the whole villa. © Rod Shelton.

Figure 4.5. The front of the villa including the veranda (from the east). © Rod Shelton.

Figure 4.6. The audience chamber. © Rod Shelton

The audience chamber (Figure 4.6.) would have been the first proper room which visitors to the villa encountered, having climbed the central staircase and crossed the veranda. Much of the mosaic depicted here is still preserved in situ (see Figure 3.1.). Visitors would have entered through the curtained doorway (just showing at the bottom right of this image and the evidence for which is referred to on page 26) and stepped onto the plain border of red tesserae. From there, they were afforded a direct view of the two personified seasons (Summer and Autumn) which probably both had harvest-related attributes and were therefore directly connected to the agricultural activities and success of the estate (see discussion on page 27). As the south-west season is missing in the original mosaic, here the artist has duplicated the image of Summer.

To enjoy the central panel of Bellerophon, visitors would have to walk around the outside of the mosaic, probably in a clockwise motion (see page 26) and then stand on the chequerboard mosaic, looking back towards the entrance through which they had just passed. Before turning to admire Bellerophon, they may have caught a glimpse of the Europa mosaic, partially visible in the top left of Figure 4.6. but the image would be upside down as the best view was reserved for those privileged enough to be permitted into the apsidal dining room.

Additional reconstructions of the villa

Figure 4.7. The audience chamber, with the apsidal dining room beyond. © Rod Shelton.

Figure 4.7. exemplifies how the interior architecture enabled the wealthy owner to differentiate between different classes of visitors (see page 35). Tenants and farmworkers probably never proceeded beyond the audience chamber and its large-scale mosaic. At the threshold of the apsidal dining room which boasted the smaller (and more exclusive) Europa mosaic, a 23cm step emphasised that only invitees should venture beyond.

The wall-paintings depicted in the model's apsidal dining room are unsupported by evidence found at Lullingstone and are based instead on wall-paintings excavated in Pompeii. However, it is quite feasible (given the evidence that we have for other parts of Lullingstone's interior) that the owner would have been keen to emulate the homes of the wealthy Roman élite with similarly Classical themed images on his walls as well as his floors. This would be another opportunity to express his *paideia* (see page 2).

Chapter Two describes the importance in Roman society of having one's own bath complex in order to impress business colleagues as well as friends. The Lullingstone owner made the most of the landscape to construct his baths at the south of the villa, which was on a lower level than the rest of the building (see page 9 and Figures 2.5. and 2.6.).

Figure 4.8. The bath complex at the south of the villa, including the well. © Rod Shelton.

Figure 4.9. The house-church at the north of the villa. © Rod Shelton

From left to right in Figure 4.8. we can see the fuel store, the hot room (*caldarium*) with hot plunge bath, the warm room (*tepidarium*), the cold room (*frigidarium*) and the cold plunge bath. The well to the south of the villa is now housed and visible within the cover building which was built around the archaeological remains of the villa.

The house-church is believed to have consisted of a series of rooms through which visitors coming to worship would have passed. As shown in Figure 4.9., the largest room probably contained the wall-paintings which are now on display at the British Museum, showing figures in the 'orantes' pose (see Figure 1.2).

As the house-church was at the north end of the villa, visitors could have attended for worship without having to access the central reception rooms of the villa (see Figures 4.4. and 4.7.).

As also shown in Figure 2.9, and here in Figure 4.10., the Deep Room was at underground level. It appeared to be a cult room dedicated to the water-nymphs who were depicted in a niched wall-painting. As discussed on page 1, the Christian house-church was believed to have been built above, and used simultaneously as, this pagan cult room. So far this is a unique discovery in Roman Britain, if not the empire.

Figure 4.10. The Deep Room seen beneath the floorboards of the room above it. © Rod Shelton.

Summary of reconstructions

It is hoped that these additional images will enable the reader better to visualise Lullingstone Roman Villa at the time of its occupancy in the late third and fourth centuries AD. The images complement and can be cross-referenced with those in the first three chapters of this book. Each of them has individual merits and different strengths. While they do not profess to be exact historical replicas, they contribute greatly to the aims of this book, namely, to demonstrate the claims Lullingstone's inhabitants were making about their status and cultural identity and also to bring to life for the modern reader a beautiful c.1,600-year-old villa which was, first and foremost, someone's home.

Chapter Five
Conclusion

By examining the evidence from Lullingstone in new ways, this book has demonstrated that Wallace-Hadrill and Scott's approaches can be combined to help us understand the owner's motives and the aspirational claims he was making. He was a likely member of the civic and/or provincial élite and we can expect that he had sensitivity to the landscape setting, architecture and choice of decoration. He used the exterior and the interior of his villa to convey his values. Monumentality and visibility were recurring phenomena through Roman architecture and these were adopted with great effect at Lullingstone.

We have seen how the ensemble of the architecture, the mosaics and the exterior space worked to persuade visitors of the owner's wealth and status. This included his right and ability to tame the landscape. The scale of his house was important but so was the organisation of its interior space. The richly decorated rooms were used for a wide range of visitors and access to them was closely controlled. As a plausible scenario, the local élite would have enjoyed *convivia* looking out from the innermost apse whilst tenants and workers on their dutiful morning visits to the audience chamber would have merely glimpsed the elaborate inscribed mosaic.

The choices of mosaics provide compelling evidence of a traditional Classical education and sophisticated knowledge of Virgil and Ovid. The inscription is a remarkable paradigm of *paideia*. For Mediterranean visitors, the mosaics and inscription would be recognisable as inherent parts of their own education and cultural aspirations. They may have been sensitive to the provincial style of the mosaics but recognised the allusions nonetheless. Even the architectural setting was a reinforcement of this desire to embrace Roman style, as the apsidal dining room was a feature of late antique houses across the Empire.[1] However, the Lullingstone patron went one step further than most patrons in combining verbal and visual displays of his aspirations.[2]

Literary sources (Pliny the Younger, Sidonius Apollinaris and Ausonius) written by other villa-owners reveal much of their ambitions, which were both material and intellectual. The sources also indicate the importance of the landscape setting.[3] In boasting of his own grand estate, Sidonius praised his neighbours' residences (*Epistulae* 2.2; 8.4). This indicates the closely linked network of these villa-owners - their villas had the potential to be compared with each other's, and thus were designed to be so. Lullingstone was one of a group of affluent villas representing foci of productive agricultural estates[4] which had formed along the River Darent, within easy reach of London, enabling the villa-owners to exploit the army and administration's market demands. The villa-owners would have shared the same social network and probably

---

[1] Ellis 1995.
[2] Leader-Newby 2007: 190-3.
[3] Scott 2000: 111.
[4] Scott 2004: 55.

entertained each other (as well as extra-provincial visitors, given their proximity to London) in their lavish homes.

The villas provided a stage for social, economic and political life. The Lullingstone owner acted out his role as a powerful and influential individual, displaying his cultural identity and status. There would have been a distinct social division between the Darent Valley network of élite villa-owners and the workforce living on their estates. The high visibility of the grand villas in their landscape setting simply reinforced the gulf between the educated, wealthy élite and those outside their close-knit circle.[5] This gulf emphasised the difference in the resources at their disposal and the villa-owners' ability to modify the landscape and perform a role as a patron and host.

Exploration of the site on foot enables us to evaluate the topography and demonstrate the visibility of the villa in its landscape setting. Future research could encompass GIS surveys and a formal viewshed analysis[6] to enable us to assess the wider landscape of the villa and its ancillary buildings, particularly to characterise the view of and from the villa more precisely. Re-excavation of the granary could also address the imbalance in our modern focus on *otium* and help us better to understand the economic basis of power.

The Lullingstone owner adopted and adapted the traditional Classical motifs to further his social and political purposes. He used terracing in the landscape to theatrical effect, a trick mirrored by his villa's interior architecture with its use of a step onto the apse-cum-stage where he regularly performed for a broad spectrum of visitors. Although there are many examples of grand and affluent villas in this period, such villa sites were exceptional. It was the owners of these villas, including Lullingstone, who could afford monumental temple-mausoleums, grand granaries and luxurious mosaics. We are fortunate that the landscape which served the owner's purposes in Roman times has also performed a service for us in the years since, by washing soil and debris downhill and thus preserving much of the villa and its mosaics for us to explore 1,600 years later.

---

[5] Scott 2000: 168.

[6] Following Eckardt et al. 2009.

Bibliography

Barbet, A. and M. Fuchs (2008) *Les Murs Murmurent. Graffitis Gallo-Romains: Catalogue de l'Exposition créée au Musée Romain de Lausanne-Vidy*. Gollion.

Barrett, A. A. (1978) 'Knowledge of the literary classics in Roman Britain', *Britannia* 9: 307-13.

Beeson, A. (2018) 'The Boxford Bellerophon mosaic', *Bulletin of the Association for Roman Archaeology* 24: 86-92.

Bergmann, B. (1991) 'Painted perspectives of a villa visit: landscape as status and metaphor' in E.K. Gazda (ed.), *Roman Art in the Private Sphere: New Perspectives on the Architecture and Décor of the Domus, Villa and Insula*. Ann Arbor: 49-70.

Black, E. W. (1987) *The Roman Villas of South-East England*. Oxford.

Bowden, H. and J. Pearce (2017) 'Seeing the gods in Roman London', in Quash, B., A. Rosen and C. Reddaway (eds.), *Visualising a Sacred City: London, Art and Religion*. London: 19-38.

Bowman, A.K., J.D. Thomas and R.S.O. Tomlin (2010) 'The Vindolanda writing-tablets (Tabulae Vinolandenses IV, Part 1)', *Britannia* 41: 187-224.

Casey, P.J. (1994) *Carausius and Allectus: The British Usurpers*. London.

Cosh, S. R. (2001) 'Seasonal dining-rooms in Romano-British houses', *Brittania* 32: 219-42.

Cosh, S.R. (2016) 'The Lullingstone Mosaic Inscription - A Parody of Martial?', *Brittania* 47: 262-66.

Cunliffe, B. (2013) *The Roman Villa at Brading, Isle of Wight: the excavations of 2008-10*. Oxford.

De la Bédoyère, G. (2001) *The Buildings of Roman Britain*. Stroud.

Dunbabin, K. M. D. (1994) 'The use of private space', in *La ciutat en el món romà: actes/ XIV Congrés Internacional d'Arqueologia Clàssica*. Tarragona: 165-76.

Dunbabin, K. M. D. (1999) *Mosaics of the Greek and Roman World*. Cambridge.

Eckardt, H., P. Brewer, S. Hay and S. Poppy (2009) 'Roman barrows and their landscape context: a GIS case study at Bartlow, Cambridgeshire', *Britannia* 40: 65-98.

Ellis, S. P. (1991) 'Power, architecture and décor: how the late Roman aristocrat appeared to his guests', in E.K. Gazda (ed.), *Roman Art in the Private Sphere: New Perspectives on the Architecture and Décor of the Domus, Villa and Insula*. Ann Arbor: 117-134.

Ellis, S.P. (1995) 'Classical reception rooms in Romano-British houses', *Brittania* 26: 163-78.

Elsner, J. (1998) *Imperial Rome and Christian Triumph*. Oxford.

Elsner, J. (2007) *Roman Eyes: Visuality and Subjectivity in Art and Text*. Princeton.

Esmonde Cleary, S. (2013) *Chedworth: Life in a Roman Villa*. Stroud.

Fuchs, M. and Y. Dubois (1997) 'Peintures et graffiti à la villa romaine de Contigny, Lausanne', *Jahrbuch der Schweizerischen Gesellschaft für Ur- und Frühgeschichte* 80: 173-186.

Fulford, M. (2003) *Lullingstone Roman Villa*. London.

Henig, M. (1995) *The Art of Roman Britain*. Ann Arbor.

Henig, M. (1997) 'Art, religion and letters in a fourth-century villa: the Lullingstone villa mosaic', *Mosaic* 24: 4-7.

Henig, M. and G. Soffe (1993) 'The Thruxton Roman villa and its mosaic pavement', *Journal of the British Archaeological Association* 146: 1-28.

Hingley, R. (2004) 'Rural settlement in Roman Britain', in Todd, M. (ed.), *Companion to Roman Britain*. Oxford: 327-348.

Kruschwitz, P. (2015) *Undying Voices: The Poetry of Roman Britain*. Webpage cited below: under 'thepetrifiedmuse.blog/undying-voices'.

Lavagne, H. (2000) *Recueil général des Mosaïques de la Gaule*. Vol III.3. Paris.

Leader-Newby, R. (2007) 'Inscribed mosaics in the late Roman empire: perspectives from east and west', in Newby, Z. and R, Newby-Leader (eds.), *Art and Inscriptions in the Ancient World*. Cambridge: 179-99.

Ling, R. (1981) 'Further thoughts on fourth-century mosaics', *Britannia* 12: 292-3.

Ling, R. (1983) 'The seasons in Romano-British mosaic pavements', *Britannia* 14: 13-22.

Ling. R. (1991) 'Brading, Brantingham and York: a new look at some fourth-century mosaics', *Brittania* 22: 147-57.

Ling, R. (1997) 'Mosaics in Roman Britain: discoveries and research since 1945', *Britannia* 28: 259-95.

Ling, R. (1998) *Ancient Mosaics*. London.

Martins, C. B. (2004) *Becoming consumers: looking beyond wealth as an explanation for villa variability: perspectives from the East of England*. University of Durham.

Meates, G.W., E. Greenfield and E. Birchenough (1951) 'The Lullingstone Roman Villa', *Archaeologia Cantiana* LXIII: 144-6.

Meates, G.W., E. Greenfield and E. Birchenough (1952) 'The Lullingstone Roman Villa: Second Interim Report', *Archaeologia Cantiana* LXV: 26-78.

Meates, G.W., E. Greenfield and E. Birchenough (1953) 'The Lullingstone Roman Villa: Third Interim Report', *Archaeologia Cantiana* LXVI: 15-36.

Meates, G. W. (1955) *Lullingstone Roman Villa*. London.

Meates, G. W. (1963) *Lullingstone Roman Villa, Kent*. London.

Meates, G. W. (1979) *The Lullingstone Roman Villa Volume I - The Site*. London.

Meates, G. W. (1987) *The Lullingstone Roman Villa Volume II - The Wall Paintings and Finds*. Gloucester.

Millett, M. (1990) *The Romanization of Britain: An essay in archaeological interpretation*. Cambridge.

Millett, M. (2016) '"By small things revealed": rural settlement and society', in Millett, M., L. Revell and A. J. Moore (eds.), *Oxford Handbook of Roman Britain*. Oxford: 699-719.

Neal, D. S. (1991) *Lullingstone Roman Villa*. London.

Neal, D.S. and S. R. Cosh (2009) *Roman Mosaics of Britain. Volume III: South-East Britain Parts 1 and 2*. London.

Perring, D. (2003) '"Gnosticism" in fourth-century Britain: the Frampton mosaics reconsidered', *Britannia* 34: 97-127.

Philp, B. and M. Chenery (2006) *Lullingstone and Shoreham: Discoveries at the Roman Villa Sites 1982-86*. Kent.

Purcell, N. (1995) 'The Roman villa and the landscape of production', in Cornell, T. J. and K. Lomas (eds.), *Urban Society in Roman Italy*. London: 151-179.

Scott, S. (2000) *Art and Society in Fourth Century Britain: Villa Mosaics in Context*. Oxford.

Scott, S. (2004) 'Elites, exhibitionism and the society of the late Roman villa', in N. Christie (ed.), *Landscapes of Change: Rural Evolutions in Late Antiquity and the Early Middle Ages*. Aldershot: 39-65.

Scott, S. (2012) 'Fourth-century villas in the Coln Valley, Gloucestershire: identifying patrons and viewers', in Birk, S. and B. Poulsen (eds.), *Patrons and Viewers in Late Antiquity.* Aarhus: 189-216.

Stupperich, R. (1980) 'A reconsideration of some fourth-century mosaics', *Britannia* 11: 289-301.

Taylor, J. (2011) 'The idea of the villa: Reassessing Villa Development in South East Britain', in Roymans, N. and T. Derks (eds.), *Villa Landscapes in the Roman North.* Amsterdam: 179-194.

Tilley, C. (1994) *A Phenomenology of Landscape.* Oxford.

Tomlin, R. (1996) 'A five-acre wood in Roman Kent', in Bird, J., M.W.C. Hassall and H. Sheldon (eds.), *Interpreting Roman London: Papers in Memory of Hugh Chapman.* Oxford: 209-15.

Toynbee, J.M.C. (1964) *Art in Britain Under the Romans.* Oxford.

Wallace-Hadrill, A. (1988) 'The Social Structure of the Roman House', *Papers of the British School at Rome* 56: 43-97.

Wilson, P. (2009) *Lullingstone Roman Villa.* London.

Witts, P. (2000) 'Mosaics and room function: the evidence from some fourth-century Romano-British villas', *Britannia* 31: 291-324.

Witts, P. (2005) *Mosaics in Roman Britain: Stories in Stone.* Stroud.

Online sources

Historic England: https://historicengland.org.uk/listing/the-list/list-entry/1012965 (accessed 27/8/18).

History of York: http://www.historyofyork.org.uk/themes/roman/tombstone-of-julia-velva (accessed 28/9/18).

The Petrified Muse - Peter Kruschwitz: https://thepetrifiedmuse.blog/undying-voices/ (accessed 13/6/18).

Kent County Council: http://webapps.kent.gov.uk/KCC.HeritageMaps.Web.Sites.Public/Default.aspx (accessed 26/9/18).